FEAR OF THE DARK

EXORCISING THE GHOSTS OF RACISM THAT HAUNTED MY FAMILY

by

Francis Megahy

For Ken, Sally and Flick

And all those Megahys who can trace their ancestors
back to Barbados

Cover and Illustration Design by Sara Rivas

Thanks to Laureen Megahy and Andrew Bergman, for spotting so many textual errors; to Peter Rawley, for his invaluable help on this project, as on so many others; and to Alex and Susan, under whose roof I wrote this book

Every day you make progress. Every step may be fruitful. Yet there will stretch out before you an ever-lengthening, ever-ascending, ever-improving path. You know you will never get to the end of the journey. But this, so far from discouraging, only adds to the joy and glory of the climb.
Winston Churchill

In all affairs it's a healthy thing now and then to hang a question mark on the things you have long taken for granted.
Bertrand Russell

CONTENTS

INTRODUCTION

For many years, decades, I had a recurring dream about my father.

I was driving in a strange part of London, somewhere that was clearly London, but a part of the city I didn't know. It was a sunny day, but the light was cold and hard. Suddenly, I saw my father walking along the sidewalk toward me. He was wearing a felt hat, and a camelhair overcoat, high lapels, cut straight down with no waist, just as I always remembered him dressed in winter. He looked healthy, and vigorous.

I was excited to see him, I pulled into the curb beside him and stopped, rolling down the passenger window.

'Dad!'

He stopped, smiling a warm smile.

'Hello, son,' he said.

'We miss you,' I said, 'we miss you terribly!'

He kept that warm smile. 'I know,' he said, 'I know you do.'

I asked, 'But when are you coming back?'

He said, 'Tell your mother I'll be home soon. But now, I really have to go!'

He walked away, quickly but not hurriedly, fading away like the last shot in a movie, leaving me with so much to say, so much to ask, words that we would never exchange.

I had that dream for thirty years after his sudden death, which in truth did leave us with more to say to each other than I could ever have imagined.

How would you feel if one day you discovered, out of the blue, and quite by chance, that your father was not who you thought he was, that his whole life story as you knew it was a lie?

Would you be shocked, angry, baffled, confused? All of those things? How would you process this information, with your new knowledge of your father, and therefore, of yourself? How would you feel about your father?

This is the story of how, long after the deaths of both my father and my mother, I dealt with all those issues; how I tracked my father's real story, and discovered the convoluted tale of why he had lived a lie for most of his adult life. In discovering the truth of his life, and the reasons that made him re-invent himself, I came to a new understanding of him, a new sympathy for him, and I gained a new insight into my own life.

*

Whenever I think of my father, I smile: we just had so much fun together. When I was born, he couldn't wait to take me for a ride in his car, so on the second day of my life we went for a drive, and from that moment on, I absorbed his love of motor vehicles, an adult sickness that infects me to this day.

As I grew older, we talked endlessly about cars, about steam locomotives, about aircraft and ocean liners. When I built model aircraft, he became my willing assistant, helping me to launch them, or to get their tiny gas engines started.

I loved all things mechanical, and I became

fascinated with the London Underground. By the time I was twelve years old, I knew its history, I could draw a map of the entire 250 mile system, most of which I had explored. With one nagging exception.

Every day, I traveled the District Line from our home in East London, to school and back, but I had never been past East Ham, my home stop. I had never been to Upminster, a mysterious place at the far end of the line, way beyond the familiar outskirts of the city, as far as the train went, and I wanted to see it, to experience the bridges and tunnels and the views of other trains and new stations and check out the sidings and see how the trains were marshaled and prepared for their return journeys.

So, one day when school finished earlier than usual, I didn't get off the train at East Ham, but rode onwards, staring out of the windows, checking out all the new stations, writing down the numbers of any of the steam locomotives I saw, until I finally reached – Upminster !

At last I saw it, from that same train that had burrowed beneath London's crowded streets, wound its way through the industrial belt around the city, and finally escaped the outer edges of the metropolis, where tunnel walls were replaced by trees.

Upminster station, a routine Victorian structure, elevated above what had once been a village, might have disappointed some, but I was delighted by its archaic design and by the view it gave of what had become suburban sprawl. Who knew what lives were lived beneath those fake terra cotta tiled roofs!

I walked to the end of the platform and counted the

branches of the sidings where the District Line trains were maneuvered into the huge washing shed or re-set for their return journey. I waved to the driver of a steam engine pulling a few passenger coaches – and got a wave back. Finally, my curiosity satisfied, I crossed over the pedestrian bridge to the opposite platform and waited there to board an empty train for my return journey to East Ham.

With the careless optimism of childhood, I hadn't given a thought to warning my parents about this lengthy diversion. When I eventually got home a full two hours past my usual time, my mother was standing outside our house, glaring down the street, her arms furiously wrapped around herself. When she saw me, she shouted, 'He's here, Ken!' and my father strode out of the house, looking angry.

'Where the hell have you been!' he said.

'Ken, language!' said my mother, and turned to me with, 'Yes, what's wrong with you, Francis, not coming home! I've been worried sick!'

'She has,' he said. 'Your mother's been going out of her mind!'

She looked me over, saw that I had come to no harm, and her relief turned instantly to exasperation. 'So?' she asked. 'Where have you been?'

I said, 'I went to Upminster.'

'Upminster? What's in Upminster?'

'It's the end of the District Line,' I said.

She turned to my father, 'I think your son is mad!' she said.

'I wanted to see the end of the line, Dad.'

He nodded, biting his lip, his anger gone. We had often talked about my fascination with the

Underground; he understood my explanation and he knew that my mother didn't and probably never would.

She sighed and shook her head tiredly. 'Go on, get in the house,' she said, 'your dinner's cold, but you're going to eat it anyway!'

As I walked past her, I caught a brief glimpse of my father, reflected in one of the windows beside the front door. He was smiling. I began to turn back towards him, to smile back at him, but my mother shooed me into the house.

It was years before I understood that her anger came from her love for me, that it was her way of controlling her fear that some mishap had befallen me; this was in such contrast with my father, whose feelings for me were always clear and uncoded. So much of her love for me was expressed in a confusing way that I often didn't notice it.

I was always surprised how little my mother and I had in common. Where my father was soft-spoken and low-key, she was outgoing, loud. Where she was gregarious, never more at home than in a crowd, he kept to himself, well satisfied with this own company.

He was the person I identified with, but I had too little self-awareness to realise how much more I was like my mother. My understanding of them and of the delicate mechanism of their relationship was so poor that I could never work out why they valued each other in ways far beyond my adolescent ken.

But however puzzling I found their relationship, we always had a lot of fun as a family. From time to time, my father would suffer an attack of flatulence. With a guilty look, he'd rush across to the nearest door and start fanning the room with it. Ken!' my mother would say, adopting a scandalized tone that was never convincing, 'If you're going to do that, at least go outside!'

'The air will clear in here in just a second,' he'd reply sheepishly, and then we'd all dissolve in gales of laughter.

My father had immense benevolence and generosity of spirit, qualities that made him such a fine family doctor, and for me, a fine parent.

In my infancy, when I seemed to be on a mission to smash all the family china, my mother would fly into furious rages, but my father would smile tolerantly and say, 'He's a child, this is what children do.'

In a good-cop, bad-cop scenario, my mother would have always been the bad cop. One of her treasured possessions was a French carving knife, I suspect that it was a wedding present. Using the carving knife as a sword one day, I plunged it into an imaginary enemy. It caught in between a door and the door frame. In trying to pull it out, I broke it.

My mother became infuriated, as much because I had broken a prized possession as by my father's refusal to get angry.

'We can get another carving knife, Sally,' he said. He looked at me with a tolerant smile, which simply made her more angry.

Only the day before I had broken a 'cut-glass' vase, my mother was very big on cut-glass. She said, 'He's becoming a very destructive child!'

'That's right, Sally,' said my father. 'He's a child, so his behavior is child-like. He'll grow out of it soon enough.'

My father was easy going with me, but I always felt that there were boundaries, I wasn't sure where they were, but I always sensed that underneath the benevolence, he had a steely quality, however well he kept it under wraps. I think in the US, in his earlier life, he'd learned not to react to many things he didn't like, and had developed way more self-control than he needed to deal cheerfully with a destructive four year old.

But this was in striking contrast to how he usually treated me: not as a child, but as an adult, and that usually made me behave like one. Being taken seriously by the person I most admired in the whole world made me take myself very seriously from an early age. We shared an instinctive understanding of each other, a kind of understanding that I only achieved with my mother much later in life.

If my mother's friends who came to dinner sometimes bored my father, we'd catch each other's eye across the table, and he knew that I saw what he was thinking. He'd shoot me a small smile, and trying not to grin, I'd look away quickly before my mother saw our secret exchange.

There was always laughter in the house. My mother had a naturally instinctive sense of humor, which I was lucky enough to inherit. When she was in her eighties, one cold winter afternoon, I went to visit her in her North London flat and noticed how cold it was.

'It's freezing in here!' I said.

She told me there was a problem with the gas and that the utility company had promised to come and fix it that morning.

'But they didn't come, did they?' I said. 'I'll call

them.'

'No, you won't!' she said, 'I can do this better than you!'

She grabbed the phone and dialed the number. Within a moment, she had adopted what she thought was a convincing old lady's voice, and in a slow and weak tone, she whined, 'I'm eighty-three years old and I'm very cold, and I'm worried I'll get ill...' Seconds later she slammed the phone down, turned to me with a grin and growled, 'That'll get em here!'

In a different, quieter way, my father was funny too. At a social event, if someone made a ridiculous remark, he would turn away from the speaker, looking at my mother, tilt his head and raise one eyebrow. She would instantly frown, Don't you dare say anything! Then they would both struggle not to laugh.

They were happy with each other and their lives. They had each had the great good fortune to find a matching partner, they were by no means rich, but they had no financial anxieties, and they had a child they admired and who delighted them.

I have a treasured memory from when I was eleven: I was in the kitchen, late in the evening, using the kitchen table as a workshop to assemble one of my model aircraft. The door to the dining room was open and my parents were sitting with coffee and talking, after dinner. I wasn't listening to them, but my attention was caught when their voices suddenly dropped, and then I did I begin to listen. Out of the corner of my eye, I saw them watching me assemble the plane's intricate wing structure, and I heard my father whisper, 'Our son is really clever, isn't he, Sally...'

My mother just smiled, and they got up and walked quietly away.

My mother and father were both complex people, and not in ways that were easily read from their everyday behavior. In my father's case, the complexity came from the great secret he was hiding, a secret which stalked him relentlessly and defined his entire adult life.

During his lifetime, I didn't even know that he had a secret, and I don't think my mother knew either. I certainly had no idea that I would stumble on the truth of my father's life in my own late middle age, and yet, the burden he bore related uncannily to an issue that had been important to me all my life.

I had detested racism from my adolescence onwards. I was myself a member of a minority that was frequently derided in the England of my youth: I was Jewish. But I also have an Irish surname and at least since the sixteenth century, the English have harbored a lurking animosity towards the Irish.

The concept of an Irish Jew seemed so strange to most English people that those who thought I was Irish, thought that I couldn't possibly be Jewish, so they would freely utter anti-Semitic remarks in my presence. Those who knew that I was Jewish were equally sure that I couldn't be Irish, and felt equally free to despise and disparage the Irish in front of me.

For most of my youth, those were the limits of my involvement in any questions of race. And indeed, that was enough – enough for me to get into childhood fights, teenage shouting matches, and robust adult debates. It was also enough, I now admit to my shame, to make me conceal my Jewish origins on occasion.

It was surprising that anti-Semitism made me so angry, because I scarcely identified with other Jews; indeed, I had my own mixed feelings about them. I didn't know it at the time, but now I know that those feelings came as much from the social class of the Jews I knew early in my life, as from their Jewishness.

My father was from Canada, and the whole of his family was in North America. The Jewish side of my family, which was consequently pretty much the only family I had, was lower class; among them you wouldn't find any of the Jewish stereotypes of virtuoso musicians, prolific novelists, big-time entrepreneurs or erudite academics. My uncles and cousins were street-traders, small shopkeepers, men who had little education, and lived on their wits. They never paid retail for anything, did well enough in the world, and they mostly succeeded in their greatest ambition: to make very sure that their children were better educated and had better lives.

I could discern no pattern in my Jewish family's lives or attitudes that synchronized with my father's. He was from the professional class, a doctor, traveled, educated, urbane. But those apparently profound differences had not prevented him from bonding with the lower class family he had married into. I was always mystified by that bond, I was the one who had a problem with it, a problem that clouded my relationship with my mother until well after my father's death.

*

Have my discoveries about my father's life made

me especially sensitive to questions of race?

I don't believe so, because although I didn't know it, my father's life and mine always weaved their way in and out of the shadows of racism. This was true of my life in Britain, even before I came to the US, even before I found out my father's true identity, and consequently, my own.

In an America in which polls routinely show that more than 1 in 6 Americans believe that a black man is 'not yet' suitable to be the President, an America in which after one year in office Barack Obama's approval rating was the lowest of any President for thirty years [1], it's scarcely surprising that I have never lost my loathing for racism.

It seems hardly possible after the acrimony following Obama's 2008 election victory, after the attacks on him during the Health care Reform debate in 2009, during the Debt crisis in 2011, and after the bitter election campaign of 2012, but I still meet people who accept the fantasy that race and racism are no longer deeply ingrained in the American consciousness, and that the election of a black President has consigned this issue to the past. These people are always white.

A 2012 survey revealed that in two states that were former strongholds of slavery, and which also regularly rank at the bottom of the nation's education statistics, Alabama and Mississippi, over 50% of Republican voters believed that Obama is a Muslim and a staggering 25% believed that his parents' interracial marriage should have been illegal [2].

If my father could magically come back to life today, he would not find a country entirely transformed. No black person can doubt that racism is alive and well in the US today, and that indeed, it's being reinforced in some surprising ways.

There's discrimination even in the use of the word 'race' itself. With the exception of some communities who feel themselves threatened by Hispanic immigration or Asian academic excellence, 'race' always refers to black people. The word is usually just a polished veneer that enables people to avoid in public the harsher, uglier terms they use in private.

Intense feelings about race are nothing new in the US: ask any American who describes themselves as 'Scots Irish'. In their time, Italian immigrants were also the target of racism and its cruel jokes, as were the Poles. Now, it's usually Hispanics, as in:

'What do you say to a Mexican in a Ferrari?'

'Stop thief!'

Today, I marvel at the hostility to Hispanic immigrants from entire groups of people whose own ancestors, a mere hundred years ago, were themselves illiterate peasants, fleeing from a life of hard agricultural labor on the Russian steppes, in the Irish bogs, or from the depredations and confusions of savage European wars. How disappointing it is that those Americans who so recently struggled up the ladder into the great vessel of opportunity have always been so quick to scorn the next wave of unfortunates attempting to climb up after them!

The idea of a melting pot is so attractive, a world in which all our skin tones and prejudices have melded into one harmonious entity – so attractive, and yet apparently an elusive fantasy. I first began to understand this in the early 60's, long before I set foot in the US, when talking to an American friend in London, Armando Del Torto, an academic. He was looking for a job back home, and we had just had dinner with a visiting friend of his, the Dean of a California college.

'Can't your friend fix you up with a job at his university?' I asked.

Armando's answer surprised me, he said, 'No, there's already a couple of Italian-Americans on the faculty.'

At that time, like most Europeans, I still thought of Americans simply as Americans – no hyphenated qualification to that description required. But my illusion that the US was a melting-pot didn't survive greater exposure to American reality. On my early visits to the US, I'd meet people who would describe themselves as Italian-Americans, or Polish-Americans, or list a bizarre pot-pourri of races as in, 'I'm part-German, and one of my grandfathers was English, and there's even some Cherokee in my background!'

Since I was born and raised in a country where 90% of the population can still trace its ancestry back hundreds of years, to the point where boredom stops the search, I was astonished to find how finely attuned Americans are to the issue of origin. You could hardly blame me for thinking that unless you're a dead shot with a bow and arrow, you're not really 'American' at all!

And that brings us to the real divide in American society, the one the United States has struggled with since the Emancipation Proclamation, and which so-called African-Americans still struggle with: the unique divide between those who came here of their own free will, as endless waves of immigrants have, as I did myself, and as my father did – and those whom slavery dragged here, kicking and screaming. The great irony is that a country to which the Pilgrims proclaimed they had fled in search of some kind of freedom, so quickly became the nation which robbed the slaves not only of their tangible, physical freedom, but far more significantly, also stole their identity. How many black Americans today can tell you where in Africa they came from, from which tribe, what was their native language, their staple diet?

Part of Obama's significance is that he's a rare combination of African and American; his African antecedents are not mysteriously buried in the incomplete records of slave plantations, but directly from Africa. Of course, he has experienced racism, but he has experienced it through a different sense of his own identity and through a different sensibility from the average African-American. This is such an incendiary subject that commentators rarely make this analysis.

*

After a century and a half of continuing discrimination and bigotry, the descendants of the reluctant slaves sadly manifest their identity in a welter of negative statistics: poor educational achievements, a high crime rate, a steady out-of-wedlock birth rate. In all of those categories, blacks in America who are not of US slave descent fare much better.

Those blacks who have recently come from Africa

of their own accord, and even those of slave descent from the Caribbean like my father, rarely identify with 'African-Americans'. I recall an African friend virtually ignoring an amiable greeting in a New York bar, from some cheerful black Americans.

'Why don't you want to speak to those guys?' I asked him quietly.

'Why should I?' he shrugged. 'Just because I'm black? I'm an African, man! I'm a Yoruba from Nigeria. I know who I am, and they don't have a clue who they are!'

Ghetto experiences and rap music, talk of 'gangstas' and 'ho's', roused no feelings of solidarity in this Harvard and Oxford graduate. Was it, I wondered, simply a matter of class? His grandfather in Nigeria was a chief, and no way was his skin color going to make him think of himself as a second class citizen.

Not that he was protected from the slurs and slights of racists. As a senior, but still very youthful executive of an international bank, he had a meeting one morning with a group of borrowers.

My African friend arrived in the boardroom, to find one of the borrowers, a white man of about forty, already there, shuffling through a vast pile of documents. Hardly looking at the young black man, he said, 'Photocopy these, would you!' and handed him a huge sheaf of papers.

My friend simply nodded and went to copy the documents. When he returned some 15 minutes later, the chairs around the table were filled by the rest of the borrowers. He gave the copies to the man who had asked for them, and then took his seat at the head of the table. 'Good morning, ladies and gentleman,' he said. 'Welcome to the International Bank.'

The man who had so brusquely asked him to make the copies, blushed bright red. Telling me the story, my friend laughed. I wonder if my father would have laughed at that; I'm damn sure that no American-born descendant of a slave would have found the situation remotely funny.

But I shared an incident with my African friend that not even he was able to laugh at. One evening after a fine dinner at his expense in a ritzy Tribeca restaurant, he gave me a ride back to my hotel in his rented limousine. He got out of the car to say goodnight. As we exchanged a friendly hug, a white man walking past snarled at me, 'Nigger lover!'

'Just a drunken asshole,' said my friend, but a congenial evening had finished on a note of tarnishing bitterness. I wondered how many such slights a man can endure, even a man like my father, with a strong and proud separate sense of identity.

Recalling small incidents like that gives me a tiny window, a fractional glimpse, into the way my father must have felt a hundred years ago when he arrived in the US from a Caribbean island where he was a member of an educated elite, and found himself instantly identified as 'African Colored' and immediately demoted to a lower order of humanity.

Before I heard Martin Luther King's iconic remark about judging a man not by the color of his skin, but by the content of his character, long, long before I knew I had a stake in the matter, racism both baffled and enraged me.

Was it my membership in my own frequently-derided ethnic minority, the Jews? Or had I simply retained a small child's naive concept of fairness?

Long before I knew the truth about my father, my work had often reflected my interest in the issue of race: I had made documentaries about the gray life of Pakistani textile workers in Northern England; portraying the struggles of the Hispanic community in East Los Angeles; and about a murder trial in New Jersey that sent two innocent black men to prison for twenty years.

Some thirty-five years ago, when I was shooting a documentary in the backward, deserted region of the Oklahoma and Texas Panhandles, my British crew and I were stunned to see a crudely painted notice on the side of a road leading into a small town: 'Nigger Don't Let the Sun Set on Your Ass In this Town'.

On the same project, when we wanted a break one evening from the tedium of those barren small towns in the Great Plains, we were advised by a local driver we had hired, to visit the small town of Clayton, New Mexico, where there was the restored 1880's Eklund Hotel and Saloon, complete with bat-swing doors, 'Just like in a Western!' he said.

We had an excellent dinner that night in the candle-lit Victorian dining room, flirting with the pretty young waitress whose great ambition was to move to the 'big city' – Amarillo! Such a pleasant, light-hearted evening – until we walked back down the narrow main street to our car and passed a bar that looked interesting. I suggested that we go in for a drink. Our Oklahoman driver looked in through the windows and said, 'No way!'

Astonished by the vehemence of his reaction, I

asked him why not.

'Because that's a black bar, that's why not!'

I looked in the window again. 'But there's not a black person in there,' I said.

'Mexicans!' he hissed. 'They'll stab yuh soon as look at yuh!'

Although I look 100% white, questions of race have never been far from my mind. Recently, a young black man of my acquaintance, a US Navy Lieutenant, told me the following story. He got a new posting from California to Pensacola in Florida. Shortly after he arrived at the base, a fellow black officer explained to him that there are parts of Pensacola that are not safe for a black man after dark. That's post-racial America in the early twenty-first century.

Discovering the secret my father sheltered all his adult life was simply the beginning of a journey as I slowly unraveled the layers of his true story, revealing that he had an agenda controlling his every decision which I could never have suspected.

My researches shattered many of my unquestioned lifelong assumptions about myself, and revealed the reasons for actions I had undertaken intuitively, but could never quite explain to myself.

The journey I embarked on was not only a psychological one, it was also a physical one, which would take me from the north of England to Kalamazoo, to New York's Upper West Side, to Washington, Barbados and St Lucia.

My story is about slavery, about racism, which we all know is alive and well in the western world; about 'passing', the hazardous and corroding trade-off in living under an assumed identity; and about how bigotry and prejudice distorted a fine man's life, and stunted his relationship with the world at large, and in particular, with his children. Racism framed and determined my father's life as it still frames and determines the lives of millions of others, and I now know that his response to it framed and determined my life too.

*

Doctor James Kenneth Campbell Megahy
His official British Army photograph.
Taken in 1942 when he was 57

1 Discovery: My Father Was Not Canadian

More than forty years after my father's death, I was an established writer and director of documentary films, television series and independent movies. For complex reasons, some of which I have only recently understood, I had slowly begun to spend more and more time in the US, mostly in Los Angeles, which eventually became my home.

Over the course of my career in the US, I had been involved in several nearly-movies, many of them US-Canada co-productions that were intended to be shot in Canada, but all of which had eventually collapsed.

In fact, I had walked away from the last of these possibilities. I had written a screenplay very specifically tailored to Los Angeles, about how an ordinary citizen becomes a target for an organized crime boss, and in response finds himself becoming as ruthless as his tormentor.

Two producers for whom I had already made a movie liked the screenplay, they had the funds to produce the film and offered me a deal to shoot it in Vancouver. In terms of the story, that was a setting that made no sense to me, but they insisted that it had to be done there because it was so much cheaper to shoot in Canada.

I found that hard to believe, and I decided to check with the most experienced production supervisor in Vancouver, and he confirmed my feelings. He explained that there were only two ways my movie could be made at significantly lower cost than in Los Angeles. The first was if the movie had a lot of set construction, which means a lot of labour, and this project didn't: it was all to be shot on real locations. The other way was if the production qualified for the Canadian Government Subsidy, which meant that certain key personnel had to be Canadian citizens. Since I was the writer and director, my project didn't meet that condition either, and since at the time I was doing well enough not to feel any need to compromise the project, I walked away from the deal.

But several years later, when I was under financial pressure, and work was getting thin on the ground, I recalled all this and thought, well, my father was born in Canada...

At this point, although I wasn't sure of my father's exact nationality when he died, I did recall that after his death in the early 1960's I found some correspondence in his effects relating to an attempt he'd made in the late 1940's – presumably around the time he made a trip to the US and the Caribbean to see his brothers – to 'recover' his Canadian citizenship.

To make an informal check, I called one of my oldest relatives, in Manchester, England, my cousin Constance, and she said, 'Oh, yes, he was definitely Canadian.'

I reasoned that when I established his Canadian citizenship, or at least demonstrated his birth there, it might be possible to insert myself somehow into the Subsidy rules. This would greatly increase my chances of getting work as a director.

I had an old Protestant Bible in which my father had written his family tree, and from that I knew that he was born in Halifax Nova Scotia, in 1889. After downloading a form from the internet, I wrote to the Nova Scotia Government with a check for $25, asking for a copy of his birth certificate. They had suggested checking a year on each side, but a few weeks later I was surprised to get a disappointing reply: they could find no trace of my father's birth in those years.

This was certainly odd, but I knew that when he died, my mother and I thought he was 73, but we discovered that he was in fact 77. There did seem to be some confusion about his exact birth date, so I filled in another form and tried the period 1883-1887.

When that also came up negative, I wondered if he might have been born in another Canadian province. So I began filling out and sending off forms and checks to all the other Canadian provinces to try and get a copy of his birth certificate.

This process took a few months, during which I was getting on with the rest of my life, and giving only the occasional thought to my father and where he might have been born. But when eventually *all* the replies came back negative, I was very surprised and puzzled. It looked as if he had written a false place or date of birth in his family tree, and I couldn't imagine what possible reason he could have had for doing that.

For the very first time in my life, I consciously began to think critically about my father's life story and I quickly realized that although I knew the general outline of his life before he met my mother, I had hardly any details.

He had never told me his life story as a coherent narrative, rather it had emerged in pieces over the years.

The gist of it was that his father was an Irish civil engineer, who had moved with his family to Canada when my father was an infant, and that later his father got a job in Barbados, where my father went to high school; later still, they moved to New York, where he studied medicine. After he qualified, he had worked as a ship's doctor on a boat sailing up and down the Amazon, then as a visiting doctor for the British Colonial Service in St Lucia and St Vincent, and after that, in a quest for further knowledge, he had traveled to study in Britain, where he met and fell in love with my mother, changed his religion to Jewish, embraced her vast family, and lived happily ever after!

There was nothing inconsistent or suspicious about any of that, but I couldn't recall a single conversation where we had talked about any of it in detail. The few details I did know had emerged in casual mentions, as when he told me once that he had learned to ride a horse in St Lucia; the roads were virtually non-existent there, so he could only get to see his patients by boat or on horseback.

Reflecting seriously about him for the first time in my life, I also identified a vague sense that I had of some mystery, lurking in the back of my mind for years, an unacknowledged yet undeniable piece of mental bric a brac, lying around just below the surface of my consciousness, which I knew was there and was careful not to trip over.

When I told my friend Susan Weber that discovering that he wasn't Canadian had made me realize how little I knew about him, she said, 'Why didn't you ever ask him any questions?'

'I don't know, I suppose I always thought that there would be plenty of time for that.'

She shook her head. 'No, I think you did ask questions – children always ask questions. But you must have learned, without even knowing it, from the responses that you got, that there were certain subjects that were not going to be talked about.'

That just sounded so right that I began to wonder, what were the subjects that were not to be talked about, and then two specific questions came back to puzzle me again and again.

My father was a man of great quiet charm. As a doctor he had a reassuring bedside manner, while his over-riding interest in people and a lifelong fascination with the theory and practice of medicine, gave him an air of confidence that was immensely reassuring to his patients.

In social situations he felt no need to assert himself, and this quiet confidence gave him a very attractive manner. He was also a good-looking man, and my adolescence is full of recollections of my tactless Jewish family telling me, 'You're a nice boy, Francis – but you're not as good-looking as your dad, you know!' Just what you want to hear when you're fourteen.

My father and I had never developed the kind of man-to-man exchanges where we might have discussed our romantic lives. From my earliest teenage years, I always had girlfriends, and I'm sure he saw that finding romantic companions was not going to be a problem for me. But after all, this was in the early 1950's, a notably repressed era, and I may have felt embarrassed or inhibited about talking to him about my girlfriends. Whatever the reason, we never talked about Women.

I now believe that he had his own reasons for avoiding the subject. I used to think that this would have been one of the many topics we might have discussed had he not been removed from my life by sudden death, but now I was no longer so sure about that.

Either way, my father never shared any confidences with me about any romantic life he might have had before he met my mother. I knew that when they met he was over forty years old, and thus I came to my first question: was it really possible that this charming, attractive man never had any previous romantic liaisons? I found that impossible to believe.

I felt that the second question might be linked to the first, although I was not sure how.

I knew that my father had an American medical degree, and also that he had obtained another medical degree from Edinburgh University. I didn't know exactly why he had decided to go to Edinburgh, although of course, he could not have practiced medicine in Britain with his US qualifications without some further study and passing some examinations to get his certification from the British General Medical Council. As far as I knew, he had moved from the US in the 1920's, and the period didn't give me a clue as to his motivations either.

So that was the second question: why would any doctor from North America emigrate to Europe in that era? Could it have been to escape the Depression in the US? No, it was before the Depression, both in the US, and in Europe too.

Some wild speculations came to mind – had he perhaps committed a crime in the US? Or tying together the two mysteries, could he have had a previous, unhappy marriage that he had run away from...?

Those might have been speculations, but at the very least I had identified an inexplicable discrepancy in his own account of his life. He was clearly not born in Canada, so where was he born; who was he really?

*

2 Harrison College To Ellis Island

I had a few basic facts of my father's life, at least I thought they were facts.

There was one dramatic event he had described to me: when my grandfather was tempted into what my father called the Venezuela Gold Rush.

From the time of the Spanish Conquistadors and Sir Walter Raleigh, Europeans had searched South America's jungles and mountains for the fabled city of El Dorado and its reputed vast gold deposits. The fable sprang from a misunderstanding of the story of a real tribal monarch, who used to sprinkle himself with gold dust and dive from a raft into a river – but that was in Colombia.

In the late nineteenth century, rumors began to spread that the fabled city had been in the Caura River Basin, in Bolivar State in Venezuela. Thousands of miners rushed to Venezuela seeking easy riches, and one effect of that nineteenth century influx of people can be seen today in Bolivar State, the only region in Venezuela where some English is still understood and carnival traditions commonly associated with the Caribbean have been incorporated into the local folklore [3].

In fact, the area does have huge gold deposits, and the rise in the price of gold in the twenty-first century provoked a mini gold rush and the Venezuelan government is still battling unlicensed gold miners.

In that original Venezuela Gold Rush, among the hopefuls who hacked their way through the jungle, were my grandfather and a partner.

My father described how, after enduring all kinds

of privations in the jungle, the two amateur miners had accumulated a considerable fortune in gold dust and nuggets, and they set out across Venezuela's rough terrain to return to their families. But on the second morning of their journey, my grandfather woke to find that his partner – and his stash – had both vanished. He barely made it back to Canada alive. And broke.

The next information I had about my grandfather was his job in Barbados, and this was a long-term job, lasting several years, so he took his family with him. Consequently, my father went to high school in Bridgetown, the island's capital, to a school he claimed to be 'the best in the West Indies'.

Harrison College is indeed a good school *[4]*, the one which all the Prime Ministers of Barbados have attended since Independence from Britain. My father seemed to have good memories of Harrison College and spoke fondly of friends from his Barbados high school days, such as Cammy Dash and Jubie Reece.

So Harrison College seemed as good a place any to start researching, and I wrote to the Principal, asking if they had any records of my father. I got a letter back, telling me that the Megahy family had lived on Roebuck Street, that he had had a partial scholarship and had been at the school from May 4th 1896 until he graduated, in December 1903. These were at least solid facts – although they still didn't explain why the Canadian Government could find no trace of his birth.

But I knew that he had been to New York University, and I had his medical degree from that institution, and I also knew that the family had lived in New York. In fact, according to the family tree in the Protestant Bible, my grandmother had died there.

Clearly, at some time, my father, with or without his family, must have traveled from Barbados to the US.

It was more than likely that he had travelled by a boat that would have docked in New York, and that he would have been processed through US Immigration on Ellis Island, the major port of entry for all immigrants docking from east of the US between 1885 and 1927.

My next step was to examine the newly-computerized records on the Ellis Island website. I was anticipating that a lengthy and laborious search lay ahead of me, and I was astonished that, when I typed in my father's name, within seconds my computer screen was filled with the actual, hand-written manifest of his arrival in New York on the SS *Etruria* out of Bridgetown, Barbados, via Surinam, Dutch Guiana, on May 24th 1904 *[5]*.

My father had not traveled alone, he was accompanied by his father and mother, and by my great-grandmother. It seemed as if the entire Megahy family had waited until my father graduated from Harrison College and was ready to start his university studies, and had then decided to move to the US.

There were some interesting details: it was my father's first visit to the US, he was described as a 'Clerk' and had $60 on him, a fairly considerable sum at the time. My grandparents, James and Frances – my namesake – gave their ages as forty-eight and fifty-five respectively. My grandfather was listed as a 'merchant' and had $400 on him. The fourth family member was my great-grandmother, Sarah Jane Megahy, who was seventy.

None of that was very surprising – but there

certainly was a surprise, indeed a stunning surprise waiting for me: under the heading Race, all four of my family members were described as 'African Colored'. I stared at the screen, absolutely transfixed.

African. Colored. There it was in the Immigration official's handwriting. African. Colored. My father's straight hair, light skin and regular features hadn't deceived this experienced official for a moment. Of course, I knew that my father had olive skin and wasn't Anglo-Saxon, but seeing the scratchy, yet official, handwriting... I couldn't take it in, I couldn't comprehend it. *African Colored.*

My hand on the mouse was trembling; abruptly, I turned the computer off, I needed to think.

The internet had suddenly opened a door to my father's life, and at once opened up a vast gulf between the man I thought I knew and whatever was the true reality of his life and identity. I was overpowered by a torrent of questions flooding through my head: did my mother know? Why had he never told me? What race did this make me?

I had always had a sense that there was something I didn't know about him, but I didn't know what it was that I didn't know, and now, suddenly here it was, front and center. That vague, unidentified sense of mystery that had been scuttling around the back of my mind for as long as I could remember had suddenly been crystallized as the literally dark secret of his race.

This discovery that my father wasn't white shocked me not on the basis of any racism I had hidden from myself, but in the magnitude of the information he had kept from me; and I still knew only the barest facts of his heredity. I was determined to know more, but who could I ask, where could I start?

*

3 Photographic and Other Evidence

After my father's death, my mother and I cleared out the house in Chigwell and we put some of his things, a few items of no more than sentimental value, mostly old financial records, into a large cardboard box. When she died, that box was one of the things I collected from her flat and carted around with me to my various homes in London and California, although I couldn't recall if I had ever looked inside it. But now I wanted to know my father better, to be close to him, to hold some things he had held, and I went into the garage of my house in Beverly Hills to find the box.

I carried it back into the living room, a big spectacular room looking across the San Fernando Valley to the San Bernardino Mountains. It would be more than forty years since I had could have looked in that box, and all I could remember was that it held some inconsequential souvenirs of his life.

The first thing I saw when I opened it made me smile. It was almost filled by my father's old Gladstone doctor's bag, and when I picked the bag up, just the feel of the leather, its polished surface worn almost into suede, brought my memories of him back with amazing clarity, and a vivid image immediately clicked into my head of him getting out of his car, reaching for the bag.

As I slid back the brass catch, I almost felt his presence. Inside were two very familiar items, his stethoscope and thermometer, as well as a couple of pairs of eyeglasses and two pocket watches. I looked at his glasses, but they were oddly impersonal, medical artifacts, which didn't remind me of him.

The rubber hoses on the old stethoscope were hard and cracked, but when I rubbed the metal, it immediately came up shiny. I looked at the watches, one of them was gold, my father's 'best' watch. The other one was heavy, steel, with thick glass and neat black lettering on a white face; it was the one he used every day. I wound it up, and it immediately started ticking, and I put it to my ear and listened to it, just as I had when I was an infant. I smiled, remembering how he would have to ask me repeatedly to give the watch back. I always wanted to hang on to it: that watch just had a good solid, friendly feel to it.

I put the watch and the stethoscope back in the bag, and as I was about to replace the bag in the box, I saw in the bottom of it a thick sheaf of papers, old bank accounts from the 1950's, and some other legal documents about house purchases and so on, nothing of any specific interest to me. But I decided to look at them and I pulled out some of the bank statements. One showed his earnings check for the summer quarter of 1961, it was for £1,300, a pretty good sum for three months work in those days.

Idly, I took the rest of the papers out and then felt something stiffer among them, cardboard? No, it was photographs. With a sudden sense of excitement, I pulled them out; there were three of them, quite large.

One was of a man with the palest of complexions, a bony face, receding hair and very prominent ears, and from his clothes I guessed that it dated from the very earliest years of photography in the middle of the nineteenth century.

The next one showed a man of middle age, bearing a considerable resemblance to my father. But his skin was darker than my father's and he looked almost as if a sketch artist had worked on a photograph of my father, making the features more negroid, flattening the nose and broadening the lips. I was immediately struck by the fact this man's hairline receded in exactly the same shape as my father's, and the same as the man in the first photograph.

On the back was written in a hand I did not recognize, *James Megahy* [my grandfather's name], *died of cancer of the neck April 17th 1916*.

The third photograph was of a middle-aged woman, of imposing bearing, a substantial Victorian lady with her hair in a bun. Her skin, so far as I could tell, was not very dark, but again her features were definitely negroid; she looked much more black than white.

I slowly laid the photographs out next to each other on a coffee table and stared at them so long and so hard that I almost forgot to breathe.

I was astounded: I was absolutely sure that I was looking at a photograph of my great-grandfather, Robert Megahy; that the second photograph was of my grandfather, James Megahy; and the third was of his wife, after whom I was named, my grandmother, Frances.

There they were, mute but unarguable, my ancestors of mixed race. It was staggering and inescapable: my father was not white, his ancestry was clearly African,

*

**Robert Megahy,
my great-grandfather**

**James Megahy,
my grandfather**

**Frances Megahy,
my grandmother**

He had obviously carried these photographs around with him ever since he left the US, these visual links to his mother, father and grandfather, carried them around, but always kept them hidden and never displayed. I tried to imagine how difficult that must have been for him, there must have been so many times when he wanted to show them to me, and tell me, 'These people are your family, son. This is my mother, this is my father, and this is your grandfather, your blood relatives.'

But however strong his urge to share them with me might have been, his resolve to stick to his fake story must have been stronger. I had to wonder what would have happened if my mother or I had found them.

Of course, it's possible that my mother did find these photographs, and that she had decided to leave the past alone, to protect her dead husband's secret, but I doubt it. I think if that was the case, she would never have left them in that box for me to chance upon later.

Processing the information that my father had faked his identity, that he was not white, was an entirely different matter from seeing these photographs. An intellectual process abruptly became a visceral one.

The enormity of my ignorance about half of my family almost paralyzed me. These people were my own family, they had shaped my father's life as surely as he had shaped mine, but to me, they were strangers staring out from the past. What work had they done, what lives had they led?

I knew nothing about them and my feelings of regret and indeed of anger because my father had told me nothing of them began to intensify, and I became determined to find out as much about them as I could.

*

The first thing I had to accept was that the entire family tree my father had written in his Protestant bible must be a fiction – the 'African Colored' family that travelled from Barbados to the USA was definitely not Irish!

It seemed obvious, although I had no proof, that my father and his family were in fact, Barbadians, Bajans. Checking that had to be my first task – and the truth was startlingly easy to find.

After a few phone calls to the Barbados government, I was referred to a researcher, Elizabeth, who was very experienced at tracing the kind of information I needed. I sent the modest fee she requested, and waited for her report. Four weeks later, there was an e-mail from her, with attachments.

The attachments were marriage and birth certificates. I don't know what I expected, but I got a welter of information, which answered answered so many questions – and raised so many more. I now knew for sure that my white great grandfather, from Ireland, Robert Megahy, had gone to Barbados to work on the Fisher Pond sugar plantation.

Elizabeth found his marriage certificate, and it showed that on August 3rd 1853, he married Sarah Jane Forte, the daughter of a former slave on the same plantation. As a child, Sarah Jane had been a slave herself.

A birth certificate showed that Robert had a son, James Megahy. My researcher found James's marriage certificate too. In 1879, he married Frances Thorne, my grandmother. Frances, who had one white parent and one black parent, had previously been married to a man named Brewster, so my grandfather had a stepson, Norman Brewster.

But Elizabeth's biggest discovery was my father's birth certificate: on November 17th 1885 James and Frances Megahy had a son, James Kenneth Campbell Megahy. I leaned back from my computer, trying to take it all in. The Bible's family tree *was* a total fake!

My great-grandmother, my grandfather and grandmother, and my father were all born in Barbados.

*

4   Barbados, The Unique Slave Colony

My father regularly disparaged Jamaican rum and always had a bottle of Barbados Mount Gay rum in the house.

'You don't want to drink that Jamaican nonsense!' he'd say. 'This is the real stuff, man!'

In his lifetime, you couldn't buy alcohol from all over the world in your local supermarket or liquor store, and the Mount Gay rum, along with delicious fruitcake aged in rum, was regularly sent to my father by friends on the island. Since I knew he'd been to school in Barbados, none of that seemed odd, but I might have thought, since by his own account his family left Barbados around the time he was of university age, that it was unusual for a boy of no more than eighteen to have developed such a strong taste for a particular alcoholic drink. It never occurred to me that this was a bizarre kind of patriotism.

I knew that to understand my father, I would have to understand the country he came from. All I knew about Barbados was that, like so many other Caribbean islands, it was an exporter of sugar, and that it was a former slave colony, like Jamaica or the southern American states. I soon discovered that in many crucial ways, Barbados was very different from other British Caribbean slave colonies or the Southern slave states, and that it was those critical differences that had shaped, indeed distorted, the whole course of my father's life.

One of the first things I discovered about Barbados was that it had an unexpected, strange historical connection with Jews; it was due to the efforts of Jews that Barbados became the country it is today.

In the early seventeenth century, the island had been colonized by the British Government and settlers, many of whom were convicts, were shipped out to develop a tobacco farming industry. In its early years, Barbados was in effect a penal colony for the British government. Transportation [deportation] of criminals to the island was so commonplace that everyone in Britain knew the meaning of the term 'Barbado'd'.

The Barbados tobacco plantations were manned by a combination of poor whites, indentured laborers – and exiled convicts; with this cheap labor force, the island prospered. But that didn't last long; only a few decades later, when the Virginia tobacco plantations in the American colony got into full production with unpaid slave labor, they were able to undercut the Barbados product and dominate the European market.

The English tobacco planters in Barbados were faced with going out of business – or finding a new crop. At the very same time, another group of people, Jews in Brazil, who had the perfect crop, were looking for a new country where they could grow it. This was the bizarre intersection of Jewish history and Barbados history [6].

In the fifteenth century many Jews fleeing the Spanish Inquisition had simply crossed the border into Portugal. But the Portuguese did not welcome these immigrants and soon offered them a bitter choice: conversion to Christianity, or exile. Many of those who chose exile went to the Dutch colony of Recife in Brazil, where they would be safe from persecution. Their freedom was short-lived. The Portuguese soon conquered Recife, drove the Dutch out, and the Jews were once again confronted with Catholic persecution.

When the Barbados planters were searching for a new crop, they invited a Brazilian sugar merchant – a displaced Jew from Portugal – to see if the island had a suitable climate and soil for sugarcane; and when he found that it did, he was followed to the island by many other Jews from Brazil.

In their time in Brazil the Jews had become expert in nurturing and harvesting sugar cane – and also in deforestation. In only twenty years virtually all of the natural forest in Barbados was cleared.

By the middle of the seventeenth century the Jews had become a well-established community with their own synagogue – it's still there on a street in the capital, Bridgetown, named Synagogue Lane [7] .

It's one of many ironic twists in my father's life that his conversion to Judaism in his 40's would be an essential part of his false identity.

By the end of the seventeenth century, the new sugar plantations were a resounding success and Barbados had become the English crown's most valuable colony; the port of Bridgetown became, along with Boston and London, a key link in the English Atlantic world.

The impact of the sugar industry was the beginning of a series of random events which led to Barbados becoming unique among slave colonies.

Sugar cane was a much more labor-intensive crop than tobacco, and there was a limit to the amount of white labor that was available. Also, the British convicts and indentured laborers couldn't take the combination of hard physical work and a tropical climate; they burned so easily in the sun they were known locally as 'Red Legs'. So many of them died, that to keep pace with their expanding sugar business, the planters had to find another source of labor.

The unintended consequence of the conversion of the plantations from tobacco to sugar cane was a tragic extension of the slave trade. For the next half century slaves flooded into Barbados from another part of the British Empire, from West Africa. As the sugar business expanded spectacularly, so did the slave population, from around 5,700 in 1645 to almost 140,00 by 1700. There was less and less work for the expensive white indentured workers, and by 1750, more than 30,000 of them had left the island *[8]*.

This was a dramatic change in the complexion of the Barbados population from majority white to majority black. Blacks outnumbered whites by a margin of three to one and the planters became haunted by the constant fear of a slave rebellion *[9]*.

To keep their huge slave population pacified, the planters deliberately created a liberal social environment: they allowed the slaves to retain some of their African customs, particularly their Saturday night dances, and allowed them to celebrate the end of the sugarcane harvest. These 'Crop Over' festivals were held in the grounds of the plantations' great houses, and were multi-racial events, attended by both slaves and plantation managers. The festivities included drinking competitions, feasting, singing and dancing. The slaves provided the music, with simple instruments such as a fiddle, drums and triangle.

These attempts at pacification were the beginning of a major liberalization of the lives of slaves, and created an unintended social interaction between the races.

Meanwhile, the remaining poor whites on the island had become the overseers and island's police force. These poor whites, as well as some of the wealthier ones, needed more and better schools for children, and other facilities like a printing press. The use of these amenities slowly trickled down to a select few ex-slaves, the privileged number who had been freed by instructions in their owners' wills when they died.

Slowly, the planters began to understand that they had become the fortunate beneficiaries of a historical accident: the sex ratio among Barbadian slaves had become the norm, i.e., there were more women than men, a pattern that they identified in the last decades of the seventeenth century.

So, at the same time as slave families in the US were being regularly broken up and sold separately at auction to random new owners, the Barbadian planters realized that the way for them to stabilize their slave population, and to eliminate the great expense of importing slaves, was to embrace slave families, to encourage slave reproduction. It was cheaper and easier to grow their own labor force than to import it. But to make this program work, and give the slaves opportunities to create real families, they had to treat pregnant women slaves better – which meant even more liberalization.

By the beginning of the nineteenth century Barbados was the only island in the British Caribbean that was no longer dependent on fresh slave imports from Africa to maintain its population levels. This was in startling contrast to other British West Indian islands, where the mortality rate exceeded the birth rate, and where, without continually importing more slaves, their slave populations would have died out completely.

Indeed, Barbados had so little need of slave importation that when in 1807 the British Parliament proposed abolishing the slave trade – not freeing all the existing slaves, however – Barbados was the *only* slave colony that supported the proposal *[10]*.

In contrast, this was such an abhorrent proposition to the Jamaican planters, that they threatened to offer themselves to the US for protection.

The white men on Barbados had always found a way to have sex with the black women, but now, with all the unintended liberalization of slave life, there was an inevitable increase in the intermingling of the races and mixed-race Bajans became increasingly commonplace. In a further erosion of the distinctions between the races, freed slaves were permitted to own their *own* slaves and earn money by renting them out.

Barbados, by chance, was developing a society in which the demarcation between the black and white races was becoming blurred; that line was slowly replaced by a graduated hierarchy of skin color and money.

But this all became irrelevant in 1833 – some thirty years before the issue of slavery provoked the War Between the States – when the British Parliament voted to abolish slavery in all British territories. Finally, in Barbados an estimated 83,150 slaves were emancipated. Among them was an eleven year old girl, Sarah Jane Forte.

*

5 Robert Megahy, My Great-Grandfather

Thus the stage was set for the arrival from Ireland of my great-grandfather, Robert Megahy.

He was a man made by the time and place of his youth, the Ireland of the mid-nineteenth century, and it's worth looking at life there in some detail, because the conditions which made him seek his fortune elsewhere are directly responsible for my own existence. In the mid-nineteenth century, Ireland was one of the poorest countries in Europe, three-quarters of the population was illiterate, and male life expectancy was only 40.

Robert Megahy was born in 1829, just a few years before a British survey revealed that half of the rural Irish lived in one-room, window-less mud huts, with no chimneys, where an entire family would sleep on straw. The country's mass poverty had its origins in the sixteenth century, when the Pope ex-communicated the English Queen Elizabeth 1, in 1570. The Irish then claimed that as Catholics they no longer owed allegiance to the Protestant English Crown.

This was beginning of a series of rebellions which continued intermittently over the next four hundred years. The British solution to the problem of subduing the Irish was to confiscate Irish landowners' property and hand it over to new English – or particularly – Scottish settlers.

By the mid-nineteenth century, Scottish Protestants were the majority population in Ulster, the northern six counties, a population whose loyalty was not to the country they lived in, but to England. These are the deep roots of the Catholic IRA's terrorist war against the British government in the late twentieth century.

By the time Robert Megahy was born, the new foreign landlords had divided their estates into tiny plots of land, often less than ten acres, on which Irish tenants could barely scratch a living. By the time of my great-grandfather's birth, Ireland was among the most densely populated countries in Europe, and was dependent for its food supply on one single vegetable – the potato.

Potatoes, which were found in Peru by the Spanish in the sixteenth century, had reached Ireland by about 1700. Potatoes thrived so well in the damp Irish climate that a hundred years later the potato had become Ireland's staple crop. Ireland produced many other crops, but they fetched far higher prices in the market and so they were almost all exported to England.

Compared to bread, the staple food in most European countries, potatoes, which are rich in protein, carbohydrates, minerals, and vitamins, are a far more healthy diet. More than a third of the eight million Irish people survived solely on potatoes; a single fertilized acre could produce up to 12 tons of potatoes, enough to feed an family for a year. Potatoes could also be stored, lasting almost from one harvest season until the next.

Robert Megahy was descended from one of those Scottish Protestant settler families transplanted by the English to subdue the rebellious Catholic Irish. He lived in the city of Armagh, in the north eastern, more prosperous part of the country – prosperous being a relative term, because even County Armagh was dependent on the potato.

By time Robert was sixteen, he had learned to read and write, and was becoming an accomplished blacksmith. His life looked to be set on a smooth course.

Everything was fine with the potato – until his sixteenth year, 1845, when in September, leaves on potato plants suddenly turned black and then rotted. The crop had been infected by an airborne fungus which had crossed the Atlantic in ships from North America to Britain *[11]*.

One single diseased plant could infect thousands more in less than a week. The fungus spread across Ireland with horrifying rapidity, even penetrating the ground, so that when potatoes were dug up, they looked edible, but within a few days they rotted just like those on the surface.

The results were catastrophic. As the threat of famine loomed, the British government tried to intervene, buying corn from India, and handing it out from official Food Depots. It was too little, too late. But since the potato crop in Ireland had never failed for two consecutive years, the desperate population assumed that the 1846 harvest would be blight-free. This assumption turned out to be tragically wrong.

*

In 1846, the blight struck ferociously again, devouring potato fields across Ireland at a rate of fifty miles a week. With only enough healthy potatoes in the country to last one month, the threat of famine increased.

To make matters worse, there was a change of government in England; the Tories were replaced by the Whigs, a party whose philosophy was *laissez faire* – let market forces take their course. The Whigs closed the Food Depots; the new Prime Minster, Lord John Russell, announced that 'Irish property should support Irish poverty', i.e., there would be no more help from London.

But with no work to provide the Irish with the money to buy food, *laissez faire* simply multiplied the impact of the blight. By the end of September, in the west and southwest, where people had been entirely dependent on the potato, famine rapidly turned from threat to grim reality.

Desperate people began to live off wild blackberries, nettles, turnips, roots, weeds and even green grass. To avoid eviction, they sold their livestock and pawned their clothes to pay the rent. But food prices steadily rose, and even in the city of Armagh, Robert saw starving beggars staggering through the streets – and dying in them. Then winter arrived, with ferocious blizzards blanketing the country in snow and ice.

In an attempt to provide at least some money to the starving population, the reluctant Whig government in London started a program of public works; hundreds of thousands of men, women and children were paid to build stone roads to replace the country's dirt tracks. Many of the under-fed workers dropped dead on the job.

Still food prices soared, well out of reach of the public works' pay and Robert saw a level of misery he would never forget. Nicholas Cummins, a magistrate in Cork, wrote that he had *'entered some of the hovels and the scenes which presented themselves were such as no tongue or pen can convey the slightest idea of. In one, six famished and ghastly skeletons, to all appearances dead, were huddled in a corner on some filthy straw, their sole covering what seemed a ragged horse-cloth, their wretched legs hanging about, naked above the knees. I approached with horror, and found by a low moaning they were alive... In a few minutes I was surrounded by at least 200 such phantoms, such frightful specters as no words can describe, suffering either from famine or from fever. Their demonic yells are still ringing in my ears, and their horrible images are fixed upon my brain.'*

The death rate shot up – but most people died not from hunger, but from typhus, dysentery, and other infectious diseases. Robert might have been tempted to help the dying, but anyone who did was likely to become infected and die themselves. Whole families and their carers simply collapsed along the roadside and died, victims of 'Road Fever'.

When it became obvious that the public works projects had failed, and were not paying enough to feed the workers' families, the British Government shut the plan down. Their new solution was to tax the landowners to raise money to set up Soup Kitchens. But the country was going bankrupt – stores were closing everywhere, the landowners couldn't pay the new taxes, and the demand for soup far outran supplies. In Killarney, there was one soup kitchen for 10,000 people.

The severe winter continued right into the spring of 1847; successive blizzards prevented more potato planting. In the summer, the harvest was just a quarter of the normal size and any hope that the 1847 crop would save the country was crushed.

There was no way that the Soup Kitchens could feed the millions of people who had no food. The famine now began its most savage phase and the British Government was powerless to prevent a disaster on a scale never before seen in Europe.

Reports of the Irish conditions did not move the English. The London *Times* thundered, '*In no other country have men talked treason until they are hoarse, and then gone about begging sympathy from their oppressors...and in none have they repeated more humble and piteous requests for help to those whom they have previously repaid with monstrous ingratitude.*'

People killed and ate dogs which themselves had been feeding off dead bodies. But nothing helped: the Irish were dying in their homes, on the streets, and their bodies were buried in mass unmarked graves.

With chaos and destruction all around him, Robert Megahy struggled on, working as a blacksmith. But even that line of work grew scarce because the horses he worked on were also dying; their owners couldn't afford the feed to keep them alive. Robert was shocked to see how quickly people had developed a ruthless survival mentality in which every individual fended for themselves.

Ireland began to dream of escape, escape to another country. Law-abiding men who had never done anything illegal now deliberately committed crimes in order to be arrested and 'transported' to Australia. '*Even if I had chains on my legs, I would still have something to eat,*' said a newly arrested Irish teenager.

To Robert, as to his fellow-countrymen, the refuge

seemed to be America. Before the Famine, Irish immigration to the United States was around 5,000 a year. After 1845, that figure rocketed to hundreds of thousands each year; recorded arrivals during the were well over a half-million, not counting those who arrived illegally by walking in from Canada. In their thousands, the Irish sailed for America, jammed tightly into ships with no proper accommodation or food, in which so many died that they became known as Coffin Ships.

And what Robert heard about life once they had arrived in America, from the few letters which arrived back in Ireland, was not encouraging.

The poor immigrants, with no way of moving into the hinterland, stayed in the port cities where they landed. Almshouses were filled with Irish immigrants. They begged on every street.

Through the period of the Famine, nearly a million Irish arrived in the United States. Famine immigrants were the first big wave of poor refugees ever to arrive in the US, and the country was overwhelmed. Soon, no group was despised more than the Irish.

The immigrants got their roughest welcome in Boston, Massachusetts, an Anglo-Saxon city run by descendants of English Puritans, who could proudly trace their lineage back to 1620 and the *Mayflower.* Boston's population was about 115,000, but in 1847, the city was swamped by 37,000 Irish Catholic immigrants. A Boston Committee of Internal Health described the resulting Irish slum as '*a perfect hive of human beings, without comforts and mostly without common necessaries; in many cases huddled together like brutes, without regard to age or sex or sense of decency. Under such circumstances, self-respect, forethought, all the high and noble virtues soon die out, and sullen indifference and despair or disorder, intemperance and utter degradation reign supreme.'*

Where filth and overcrowding went, disease, particularly cholera, was quick to follow. Sixty percent of the Irish children born in Boston during this period didn't live to see their seventh birthday. On average, the adult Irish lived a mere six years after stepping onto American soil.

U.S. immigration records indicate that by 1850, the Irish made up 43 percent of the foreign-born population. New York now had more Irish-born citizens than Dublin.

Soon, newspaper advertisements for jobs and housing in Boston, New York and cities routinely ended with 'Positively No Irish Need Apply', while in a horrible foretaste of signs seen later in the century, after the Civil War, bars put up signs reading 'No Irish or Dogs'.

*

Back in Ireland, no family escaped the ravages of the famine. Robert's parents had been its victims, his two older brothers had died and there was no longer anything to keep him in his home country. He was an original and determined young man, and conditions in America sounded worse than those he saw around him every day. He made a radical decision: yes, he would leave his home country – but he wouldn't go to America.

Luckily, there was another escape route. In 1847, more than 280,000 Irish refugees from the famine landed in Liverpool. Most of them stayed in the city, a tidal wave of immigration which permanently transformed it, making it forever more Irish than English. *[12]*

The eighteen year old Robert Megahy had some small savings, just enough to buy passage on the two-hour boat ride to Liverpool. But there he found that England was having its own economic problems; a railway-building bubble had burst and the economy was rocked by speculators' rash commodity investments. Banks failed and well-established businesses collapsed.

Although Robert could read and write and was a skilled blacksmith, it was almost as difficult for him to find work in Britain as in Ireland. He quickly realized that he had to move on. But to where, what was left? Well, the British Empire, the Colonies.

West Africa was a possibility, but the fearsome local diseases along the coasts of Nigeria and Ghana had earned those countries the nickname of 'The White Man's Grave'. India was also problematic; the Indians' resentment of the British occupation of their country was growing and there were rumors of rebellion. Robert wanted to stay in the English-speaking world, and that left the Caribbean, and everyone knew that in the Caribbean, the most prosperous colony was Barbados.

Robert didn't want to become an indentured servant, but he had no money for a ticket to the island. He pestered shipping and colonial agents until he finally got the deal he wanted: in exchange for a free passage, he agreed to work on a sugar plantation as a manager without pay for a year. It was a tough deal, but in

Barbados – he wouldn't starve.

A brand new life in the sunshine beckoned...

*

What must my great-grandfather have thought, when he disembarked in Bridgetown, wearing his thick Irish tweeds in a humid 85 degrees, and took in the easy-going atmosphere of the island?

At the Fisher Pond Plantation, he was trained as a junior plantation manager, and quickly embraced the local lifestyle.

There certainly was no shortage of food and there was always the attraction of the free and easy sexual mores of the local women. He soon became captivated by a former slave, Sarah Jane Forte. In the slave era, white men had always had sex with female slaves, consensually or not, and they also sometimes established long-term relations with them and bought their freedom, so there was nothing unusual about white-black liaisons.

But in 1853, Robert Megahy did something which in Britain or the US at that time would have been totally out of the question – and was unusual even in Barbados: he married the young woman who was to become my great-grandmother, Sarah Jane Forte, the dark-skinned child of a slave and a white man, who had also worked on the Fisher Pond Plantation. Along with thousands of other slaves, she had been given her freedom some twenty years before, by the 1833 British Emancipation Act; and now, twelve years before the US Emancipation Proclamation, she had married a white man.

To put my great-grandparents' marriage in

perspective, over one hundred years later, in 1957, for the 'crime' of marrying someone from another race, in 29 US states both Robert and Sarah Jane could have been sent to prison for five years.

Robert continued to work as a plantation manager, and he and Sarah Jane set up their marital home in a small rented house. They had a happy marriage but alas, a short one; Robert died in 1862, but not before they had produced a son, James Megahy, my grandfather, in 1855.

James grew up to become a prosperous sugar merchant and by the age of 28, was successful and confident enough to marry a young widow, Mrs. Frances Brewster, who already had one child. They soon had two children of their own; the second of those children was my father, James Kenneth Campbell Megahy, born in 1885.

My father was born into a very different society from any existing at that time in Britain, in the Caribbean or in the US. A Barbadian black man, David Augustus Straker, who had emigrated to the US in 1880, returned to the Caribbean in 1905, and wrote a book about his journey, 'Travels to the Windward Islands'.

Among his many observations about the islands, are his descriptions of the racial and social divisions in Barbados. He wrote that *'The social distinctions of the middle and upper classes are much alike, being chiefly wealth, culture and rank. Both these classes of society in Barbados mark the refinement, culture and intelligence of the natives and is of high character. These two classes are always towards a convergence and seem inclined to blend, unless a foreign infusion of color prejudice retards the same.'*

'White women are more generally employed in stores than colored women. Colored men are also the proprietors of stores, such as hardware, dry goods, book stores and general provision stores. Many are planters and merchants and are rated among the wealthy class of the island. They live in good style having their horses and carriages and dwell in fine houses among their white neighbors of similar rank and station.' [13]

My grandfather was one of those merchants and quite well-to-do. He had raised his stepson, my father's half-brother, my Uncle Norman, as his own son, and he sent Norman to an excellent Bridgetown school, Combermere. A few short years later, he was able to send both of his own children, on partial scholarships, to the prestigious local high school, Harrison College – which was founded before Princeton or Columbia – where in class, my father sat next to the perfectly white children of the wealthiest planters on the island.

One can see that James Megahy and my grandmother, Frances, after whom I am named, were an adventurous and very ambitious couple. They were comfortably settled in Barbados, but they also had a burning ambition that their children would do better in life than they had, and they knew the route to that better life was education.

Norman wanted to be a doctor, and would soon go to Britain to study; he had used his academic excellence to get a scholarship to one of the best medical schools in Europe: Edinburgh, in Scotland. My father's natural brother, Evan, was to go to Chicago, to study at the Armor Institute, later known as 'Illinois Tech', to become an engineer, and he too later became a doctor. My father greatly admired Norman, and also wanted to be a doctor. Like his brother and half-brother, my father got a scholarship to a medical school, in his case in the US.

My great-grand mother Sarah Jane was overjoyed by these life-changing academic achievements; at the beginning of the twentieth century in Europe, it would have been remarkable for all three sons of a white working class family to become physicians. For the grandchildren of a woman who had started life as a slave, it was truly astonishing.

With Norman studying in Scotland, Evan in Chicago, and my father about to study in the US, there was nothing to keep my grandfather and grandmother in Barbados. They took a momentous decision; they would seek a new life in the United States.

They didn't want to leave my great-grandmother alone on the island, and besides, she was as adventurous as the rest of her family, so she made the great journey with them. In April 1904 the entire Megahy clan left their island paradise, where they had been near the top of the class system, and boarded the steamship *Etruria*, to travel via Surinam to New York.

They had between them some $460. It's difficult to make an accurate assessment of the value of that amount of money today, but most estimates suggest that it represents around $50,000.00 in current purchasing power. A realistic contemporary comparison is that in 1904, the minimum that the US required immigrants to have in their possession was only $25.00; so my father and his family were justifiably optimistic about their prospects in the US.

But I think they had only the sketchiest idea of what life was like in America for black people, and could not conceive the variety of surprises and shocks which awaited them there.

*

6 Back Of The Bus, Boy!

Among the few documents of my father's that I had was his graduation certificate from NYU Medical School, so at this stage in my researches, I knew the date when he entered NYU and I knew the date when he and his family left Barbados.

But those events were separated by ten years, and in that era, a medical degree took only four years: what did he do in the intervening six years?

I wondered if he had to get some kind of a work, to generate the money to pay his fees at NYU, but I could find no record of that. I decided to go back to the box of my father's papers, where I had found the photographs, perhaps there was some clue there.

Previously, I had been so absorbed by the photographs that I had only glanced quickly at the papers in the box; now I looked through them more carefully. They were mostly old financial documents and letters from his accountants. Nothing much there. But then, as I idly leafed through the pages of his bank statements, my eye was caught by a regular, recurring payment, a payment to Howard University. When I first hurriedly looked at these bank statements, I had mis-read Howard as Harvard.

Of course I had heard of Harvard, but never of Howard. Why would my father have been making regular payments to this university I had never heard of? I called Howard, in Washington, DC, and I was astonished to be told that he was a Howard Alumnus, and that the payments had been his Association membership dues. The University confirmed that he had graduated from there, as a doctor, in 1908.

I had made another extraordinary discovery: my

father had been to another university *before* he went to NYU. I couldn't imagine why.

Although he had kept his Howard degree secret, that institution clearly had some special meaning for him; I could find no trace of his membership in the NYU Alumnus Association, but he had continued to pay the Howard dues right up until he died. When I researched Howard, I got the beginnings of an idea, not of why he had attended that school, but of why he might have later gone to NYU, because the first thing I discovered about Howard was that it was a segregated university. It had been founded in 1868 for black students only, and is the oldest black medical school in the US.

When my father was at Harrison College in Bridgetown, the student body was both white and black – and like him, some shades in between. When my father entered Howard as soon as he arrived in the US, it was the first segregated institution he had ever encountered. But the unpleasant realities of his US experience started before he traveled to Washington, they started immediately he and his family disembarked from the *Etruria* on Ellis Island, where they made a shocking, life-changing discovery: in the US, they were a second class citizens.

Perhaps the Megahy family had some anecdotal knowledge of the difference between their life in Barbados and their possibilities of life in the US. They would almost certainly have known about the Emancipation Proclamation, and may have known about Reconstruction – and after all, they had moved to a country in which 750,000 men had died forty years earlier in a struggle to destroy slavery. So black people in the US were citizens with all the rights which that entailed, correct?

Well, not exactly. On 16th October, 1901, President Theodore Roosevelt had scandalized white America by inviting Booker T. Washington – the most prominent black man in America, an educator, author and political activist – to dinner at the White House. The outrage of white racists was fiercely expressed: a Memphis newspaper editorial thundered that the invitation was 'The most damnable outrage ever perpetrated by a citizen of this country!' Only three years after that 'damnable outrage', the Megahys found that they had moved to a country in which virulent racism was nothing to be ashamed of, and in which bigotry and prejudice were a part of everyday life and had become more and more legitimized every year following the defeat of the Confederacy.

My father had left an environment where he was something of a star, he was en route to take up the scholarship he had won to Howard University. He was going to be a doctor, one of the first descendants of a Barbadian slave who would enter that profession. With his light skin and straight hair, and his attendance at the best high school in the Caribbean, he was an elite figure in his home country.

But when he saw the US Immigration officer on Ellis Island write out his log on that fateful May day in 1904, he knew with a sinking feeling that in this new country, he was nothing more than just another 'African Colored'.

Arriving on the fabled shores of the US was an intense experience for new immigrants: before them lay all the exciting possibilities of life in what was literally known as the 'promised land'. But any excitement the Megahy family might have felt in the Ellis Island processing facility was thoroughly curbed by the shock of being classified as African Colored.

If my father had any delusion that *African Colored* were merely words written on a document, which would have little meaning at street level, he would quickly find otherwise. From now on, the eighteen year old student would always wonder if the content of his character could overwhelm the color of his skin.

In the rigidly segregated society of the United States, where virtually all vestiges of dignity and civil rights that had been granted to slaves after the end of the Civil War had been systematically wrested from them by white bigots, this was simply the merest shadow of the humiliations to come.

The shock of my father's arrival in the US was a major turning point for him, the episode that would determine the whole course of his life, and so it's worth looking closely at the racial environment he found himself in. That environment had changed drastically in the 40 years since Reconstruction.

Reconstruction had been a serious and sincere attempt by the winners of the War, to create a level playing field between the former slaves and white Americans. But the losers of the War, the Southern States, never accepted that concept; in many cases they still haven't. The expression of bigotry might have been marginalized legally by the Emancipation Declaration – but the way Southern whites thought and felt about the former slaves had hardly changed.

At first, much was accomplished by the winners: former slaves began to prosper, to vote, and to become elected to political office. But even those black men – they were all men, of course – who managed to become elected to Congress, continued to be the victims of slights, insults and abuse. En route to Washington to start his service in 1869, the first black Member, Joseph Rainey of South Carolina, was thrown out of a hotel dining room. His South Carolina colleague, Congressman Robert Elliott, was refused service in a railroad station restaurant. In his first speech to the House, Rainey said, 'When myself and my colleagues shall leave these Halls and turn our footsteps toward our southern homes, we know not that the assassin may await our coming, as marked for his vengeance.'

The insults – and threats – which these black Congressmen suffered came not only from the public at large, but also from other Members, as when a white Virginia Democrat stood up and said that he was not addressing his black colleagues, but 'the white gentlemen' in the House. If this was the way that Congressmen were treated, what could my father and his family expect?

Gains such as election to Congress were a temporary illusion, and not a guide to where the country was headed in race relations. Within a few years of the ending of the War, Southern bigots were doing everything they could, both legally and by intimidation, to render the Emancipation Proclamation meaningless.

President Grant countered the terrible treatment meted out to the Southern blacks – especially by the Ku Ku Klan in South Carolina – by passing three key statues: the Enforcement Act of 1870, which destroyed the Klan in South Carolina for forty-five years; the Fifteenth Amendment of 1871, which by stating that voting rights could not be denied or abridged based on 'race, color, or previous condition of servitude', derailed the Southern whites' determination to disenfranchise the blacks; and the 1875 Civil Rights Act, which guaranteed all Americans access to public facilities such as restaurants, theaters, trains and other public transportation, and protected the right to serve on juries.

Using these acts, Grant exercised the power of the Federal Government to send troops to protect and support Southern blacks whenever it was necessary. But all those efforts were set aside with the 1877 election of President Rutherford B. Hayes, whose abandonment of the concept of federal intervention to protect the rights of black citizens in the South, sounded the death knell for Reconstruction. Henceforth, the fate of the former slaves would be determined by local white populations; and in 1883 the 1875 Civil Rights Act was itself overturned by the Supreme Court.

In a self-deluding perversion of the English language worthy of George Orwell's Newspeak, white Southerners described their efforts to rip away the former slaves' rights gained through the Civil War, as 'Redemption'.

In 1890, Mississippi's constitutional convention disenfranchised black voters, beginning the process of destroying blacks' right to vote. By 1900, the work of the Southern states' constitutional conventions had substantially completed that process. In Louisiana, where there had been more than 130,000 black voters, there were now only 6,000. Alabama, which used to have 181,000, was down to 3,000. Even if the Megahys became American citizens, they were very unlikely to acquire the right to vote.

Nor could they look to the Supreme Court for help; it had been complicit in destroying the freedoms blacks had gained, for example, in its renowned ruling in *Plessy* v. *Ferguson* in 1896. Homer Plessy, a Creole from New Orleans, had challenged the new Louisiana Separate Car law by sitting in a 'whites only' railroad car. In a profound defeat for civil rights, a seven-man majority on the Court decided that *apartheid* was legal – separate facilities for whites and blacks were henceforth Constitutional, so long as those facilities were equal.

The Court eventually invalidated the Emancipation Proclamation, the Enforcement Act of 1870, the Fifteenth Amendment of 1871, and the 1875 Civil Rights Act, virtually completing the restoration of the former slaves to the status that Southern whites believed was appropriate to them: a sham citizenship without any civil rights.

All of this was compounded by the 1913 election of the first Southern-born president since Reconstruction, the racist Woodrow Wilson.

Robert Smalls, a former slave who had distinguished himself during the war by stealing a Confederate gunboat and delivering it to the Union side, became a South Carolina Congressman in 1875, after which he served five terms. At the time when my father reached the United States, Robert Smalls was still in public life; he had a good job as a Customs Officer in Beaufort, South Carolina. That job ended abruptly in 1913, when he was removed in a Woodrow Wilson-ordered purge of blacks from the federal bureaucracy.

But long before that, select communities had begun their own purges, the 'ethnic cleansing' of former slaves from their towns. This was a national guilty secret, which was not even known until 2007, when David Slone's groundbreaking book, [14] *Buried in the Bitter Waters*, revealed that over a period of some 50 years after the Civil War, small towns, mostly in the South, but also in other parts of the country, spontaneously drove every single black from their community.

When Kenneth Megahy stepped off the *Etruria*, did he know how dangerous his new country was? By 1905, the murder of black men could almost be described as commonplace. In the fifty years after 1880, a black man was murdered by a white mob nearly every week in every year.

A great deal has been written about lynching, but just in case anyone whose image of lynching comes from Hollywood movies, and has the misconception that lynching was simply a matter of hanging the unfortunate victim, it's worth going into some detail about what it actually consisted of.

Thirty percent of all the men – and boys – who were lynched were accused of sexual assault. The alleged rapist – or molester – would be brought face to face with his victim, who dare not jeopardize her family's honor by denial or uncertainty. In the preliminary rituals of mutilation, the condemned man would be beaten, slashed, whipped, and spat upon by the mob, as white women and children, encouraged by the ringleaders, worked themselves into a frenzy. Before reaching the place of execution, as he moved through a homicidal gauntlet of spectators, the lynchee's ears, nose, fingers, and sometimes genitals would be slashed or cut away. The final burning of the victim was timed for maximizing community participation and group sadism. His flesh would be whipped into welts or blow-torched, and he was often be kept alive so as not to disappoint any late arrivals.

In *Time* magazine, a contemporary eyewitness described the typical denouement of a double lynching in the Mississippi Delta in 1937:

Both men continued to swear their innocence, but McDaniels ultimately broke down, his screams sending children scurrying to their mothers' sides. Once he'd confessed to the crime he was shot to death. Townes had his eyes gouged out with an ice pick and then was slowly roasted with the torch until he, too, agreed to confess. When he finally uttered the words the mob wanted to hear, he was doused with gasoline and set afire.[15]

Souvenir hunters would often fight over severed genitals and charred strips of flesh.

Even when blacks were not being driven out of town or murdered, their lives were rigidly if informally circumscribed by what was known as *Jim Crow Etiquette. [16]*

My father was expected, as an 'African Colored', to obey a specific code of conduct, which would govern all his actions, manners, attitudes and words when in the presence of whites. He had to learn this code well; breaking it at the wrong time in the wrong town could cost a black man his life.

Blacks had to refer to white males in positions of authority as 'Boss' or 'Cap'n'. Even the children of a white employer or a prominent white person might be called 'Massa,' to show special respect. All black men, on the other hand, were called by their first names or referred to as 'Boy'. The word 'nigger' was always used, unless it was the word 'negro', usually corrupted by Southern accents to 'niggra'.

Addressing blacks by words denoting their inferiority was designed to reduce them to non-people. In court and in newspaper reports, the press usually adopted the gender-neutral term 'Negro,' thus an accident report might read: 'Rescuers discovered that two women, three men, and five Negroes were killed in the accident.'

Black women were addressed as 'Auntie' or 'girl', but never as 'Miss' or 'Mrs'. Black servants and acquaintances could call white women by their first names but they had to add the word 'Miss', as in 'Miss Coral'.

Blacks and whites could meet and talk on the street, but Jim Crow Etiquette meant that blacks had to be agreeable and never challenge a white person – even if they were wrong about something. Blacks had to step off the sidewalk when meeting whites or walk on the outer edge of the sidewalk to 'give whites the wall.'

A black person could never behave as an the equal of a white; when talking to a white person, black men were expected to remove their hats. Correspondingly, whites who were too friendly or casual with blacks were likely to be called 'nigger lovers.' As noted earlier, this epithet was screamed at me on Manhattan's Upper West Side only a few years ago.

Blacks and whites could not eat together in public. Blacks were only allowed into a restaurant to buy or order take-out food. Even then, black customers weren't allowed to use the restaurants' knives and forks or plates or dishes; if they did, white customers wouldn't use them later.

Clothing stores didn't allow blacks to try on clothing, because white customers wouldn't buy clothes previously tried on by blacks. Some stores did allow blacks to put on clothing over their own clothes or to try on hats over a cloth scarf on their heads. They couldn't try shoes on, but some stores allowed exact measurements to be made.

Many public places like parks and entertainment centers excluded blacks altogether after 1890, often by law if not by custom. Venice Beach in California was segregated until the late 1920's. As with the Irish immigrants from the Potato Famine, signs were often posted equating blacks with animals: 'Negroes and dogs not allowed.'

In some communities blacks could attend public performances, but only by using separate entrances in the back or an alley. In public halls, theaters, and movie theaters, they always sat upstairs in the so-called 'nigger heaven' or 'buzzard roost.' Even state fairs would have a 'colored day'.

Law separated the races in public transportation, but local communities usually determined how those laws were enforced. Some cities made blacks sit in the back of streetcars, but others wanted them up front – where they could be watched by the car's operator. Motormen or conductors were not allowed to help black women with bags or parcels.

Blacks were *always* expected to give up their seats to white passengers in rush hours. On Pullman Sleeping cars on trains, all the black porters were called 'boy'. Blacks were rarely allowed to eat in railroad dining cars – and if they were, a curtain had to separate any 'colored tables' from the rest of the car.

Some towns required blacks and whites to use separate entrances to civic buildings. Although no laws regulated priority in stores, white clerks in stores and ticket agents always served white customers first.

The pettiness of these rules drove my father crazy – but he could say nothing.

State and local tax revenues were allocated as unequally and separately as toilet facilities. In Mississippi, each white child's education was allocated $22.25 from the state budget – each black got $2.00. In rural areas, when planting and harvesting time came, the sparse black school facilities were simply shut down.

Even in the US Army, the Jim Crow Etiquette prevailed. As recently as World War Two, in spite of a serious shortage of nurses, the only white servicemen whom black nurses could treat were German Prisoners of War – until the First Lady, Eleanor Roosevelt, intervened and forced the Pentagon to allow black nurses to care for white American soldiers too.

The whole intent of the Jim Crow Etiquette – what a genteel name the white racists had selected for such a pernicious practice! – had one simple objective: that blacks must not merely be subservient to whites, but they must be *seen* to be subservient in their actions, speech, and manners.

Of special interest to my father, and especially

disheartening for him, the color line and the codes of racial etiquette were also strictly observed in hospitals, with separate wards for whites and blacks. If a black person needed an ambulance, no white-owned-and-operated vehicle could be used. No exceptions were allowed, however life-threatening the emergency.

My father quickly and dismayingly discovered that as an 'African Colored' medical graduate of a blacks-only university, he would never be allowed to treat white patients. This was to profoundly affect his future plans.

Sadly, this situation was not simply tolerated by whites – it was embraced by them. As late as 1960, when black singing and movie star Dorothy Dandridge was headlining in a Las Vegas casino, she took a swim in the hotel pool. Indignant white guests complained and the hotel manager was forced to order the pool to be drained and refilled with 'clean' water.

Whenever the barriers between the races began to weaken or break down – as they did during the Reconstruction era – local laws were passed supporting a racist code of behavior. If those laws were enforced without enthusiasm, whites resorted to violence against blacks to reinforce the customs and standards of behavior. Indeed, whites commonly justified lynchings and the horrible murders of blacks during the Jim Crow era as defensive actions taken in response to black violations of the color line and rules of racial etiquette.

I have gone into this great detail about the Jim Crow Etiquette because I feel that it's only by reading the details can a white person begin to imagine how my father, an idealistic 18 year old, felt when he suddenly found himself bound by these rules. And if you think that's irrelevant to present day life in the US, then let's skip ahead to the 2012 Trayvon Martin murder case, in which a self-appointed white vigilante shot and killed an unarmed 17 year old black boy, with a transparently false claim that he was acting in self-defense. *[17]*

If my father was around to hear all the black parents who came forward in the wake of Trayvon Martin's murder, and explained how they had to repeatedly school their children not simply to defer to white authority figures like cops, but also never to put their hands in their pockets in supermarkets, I'm sure he would be astounded how little progress the US has made in its treatment of the descendants of slavery.

In my father's early life, until he arrived in the US, he had always been able to use his charm, intelligence and great good looks to buffer any unpleasantness; now he found himself in a situation in which those qualities counted for nothing.

On the train from New York to DC, he had to sit in the Coloreds Only section. At drinking fountains, in bathrooms, hotels, restaurants, in every environment of ordinary life, every minute of every day it was underlined to him that now, for the first time in his life, he was a second class citizen.

He may have seethed with resentment, but he was too smart to react when whites called him 'boy', or to reveal his anger with the white children who expected him to step off the sidewalk into the mud to let them by. He may have kept his mouth shut and his face blank, but in his heart he would never accept being shouldered to the back of any line by insensitive whites.

These formative experiences, and the abruptness of his transition from the easy-going nature of the island he had left to the ever-present racial tension of the new country he had moved to, were an emotional and intellectual acid bath; a deep-rooted sense of injustice began to grow inside him, feelings that would govern the major decisions of the rest of his life.

But my father knew how intelligent he was, how charming he was, and that even white women couldn't help themselves from reacting to his beautiful dark eyes, so he smothered his anger in ambition. He was determined that his life was going to be different: he was going to become a doctor, a valued member of society, a healer, needed by everyone, whatever the color of their skin.

We will see just how that played out.

*

My father at age 21, when he was a medical
student at Howard University in Washington DC

7 Howard, Chicago And New York

Like my father, his fellow students at Howard were determined and talented – indispensable qualities for any black man who wanted to become a doctor in America in the early years of the twentieth century.

The other students may have resented the yoke of racism, but over their lifetimes they had all learned to handle it; my father's expectations and theirs were wildly different. He had to deal with racism just as they did, but their life experience and his were so different, that far from being a common bond, it divided him from them. Like many black people from Africa and from the Caribbean, right up to the present day, my father did not identify with the American ex-slaves. My father never did bond with any of the other students, never did form any close or long-lasting friendships; I never heard him speak of any friends from the US who could conceivably have been at Howard with him.

All around my father were signs of increasing social tension. As the twentieth century began, white Americans, particularly in the South, were increasingly uneasy at the political, social and business progress that had been made by many blacks. Whites were determined to maintain their superiority over blacks, and Howard and its students were highly visible symbols of 'uppity niggers'. This meant extra vigilance for my father; unlike his fellow students, he couldn't fall back on a habit of instinctively deferring to the white world; he had to constantly remember exactly what the white world expected him to do – and he'd better do it.

In his vacations from Howard, my father visited Chicago to stay with his older brother Evan, who was studying civil engineering at the prestigious Armor Institute, later known as Illinois Tech.

Chicago was still something of a Wild West Town, a railhead that had become accustomed in its early days to the undisciplined cowboys driving cattle across country right up to its slaughterhouses. Later, as the railroad was extended west, it welcomed the cowboys from the Chisum trail who arrived with the cows on cattle trains. Chicago was more open-minded than cities in the South, and the state of Illinois had enacted some of the most progressive anti-discrimination legislation in the country: school segregation was made illegal in 1874, and segregation in public accommodations was outlawed in 1885. This was one of many reasons it attracted blacks from the South; its black population was almost 40,000 by the time of my father's first visit in 1905.

My father loved big city life, but even in Chicago, despite its progressive laws, the petty humiliations of the Jim Crow Etiquette persisted. He was very surprised to find that Evan, a notably proud man, was not resisting the subservient role that white society demanded of a black man, but making the best of it.

Evan Megahy was not only working on his studies at the Armor Institute, he was already planning his next move. 'I'm going to be a doctor, like you and Norman,' he told his astonished brother.

'As well as a civil engineer?' my father asked.

'Hell, yes!' said Norman. 'I'm going to make my mark on this town!'

Already there was a growing divide between the

brothers. My father was uncertain where exactly his future lay, while Evan was already determined that he would make a go of his life in Chicago.

*

In his vacations my father also went to see his parents and his grandmother in New York, who had arrived there during a housing glut.

In the 1890s, there had been a collapse in New York real estate values, but in the time honored way of the real estate business, that was forgotten almost immediately, and a new construction boom started again in 1903. The result was an even bigger housing glut, which led quickly to an even bigger crash in values in 1904.

This worked out very well for the Megahy family. Almost as soon as they arrived in the US, they traveled to New York and, taking advantage of the low rents, driven down by the abundance of empty properties, they moved into a large twenty-five year old brownstone house, about a mile north of the fabled apartment building, the Dakota, on Central Park West. Their house was at 15, West 99th Street, a mere couple of hundred yards from Central Park, in a good white area of the city, well south of Harlem, which at that time was principally a Jewish district. The City College of New York had recently moved to Harlem, and 90% of its students were Jewish.

Walking along Broadway or Amsterdam Avenue, stopping for a coffee in the brand new Jewish deli, *Barney Greengrass*, my father felt comfortable with Jewish people, who didn't give him those careful looks, trying to analyze him racially, which he got from other whites. His feelings about the New York Jews strangely presaged his embrace of a very different Jewish community, thirty years later.

I was in Los Angeles when I discovered that my great grandmother and my grandparents had lived on the Upper West Side. The next time I went to Manhattan, I raced up to 99th Street, in a state of high excitement, camera at the ready, to see the house my family had lived in. But I was in for a major disappointment: in the 1960's, the brownstone street had been entirely demolished to make way for a huge, block-long, nondescript, red brick apartment building, which took up not only that whole street, but 100th Street as well.

I felt demolished myself, but I had a feeling that the New York Public Library would have a fine archive of old photographs of the city. For a couple of hours I sifted through their microfiche records – and my luck was in: I was thrilled to find a photograph of the actual house!

The New York of the Upper West Side was more congenial to my father than Chicago, but even in New York, there was racial tension, and that tension had surfaced in two extremely violent riots.

The Tenderloin Riot in 1901 started with two tragic misunderstandings. A black man stabbed and killed a white man he thought was propositioning his girlfriend, who was waiting for him on a street corner. But the white man was an off-duty policeman, who was trying to arrest the woman because he thought she was a prostitute. The killing of a white man by a black, even in liberal New York, instantly provoked a riot.

Whites, frequently helped by the police – angry at the death of their colleague – went on the rampage, severely beating a couple of hundred black men and women, several of whom later died from their injuries.

Four years later came the San Juan Hill Riot. This was in the area around 62nd Street, west of Amsterdam Avenue, just over thirty blocks from my grandparents' house. It was described by a *New York Times* reporter as '*probably the most lawless section of the city. A large proportion of the population consists of West Indian Negroes who are partly of Carib Blood.*'

In a spectacularly uninhibited burst of racist rhetoric, the reporter continued, '*These people represent the lowest order of civilization that I know in the most heterogeneous polyglot population of the most cosmopolitan city in the world. These West Indian Carib and half-breeds differ in appearance somewhat from the mass of negroes one sees in the North. Their hair is not kinky but long and straight. Among the colored folks [*he means American blacks*] they are called 'straight-haired coons'*... *They are instinctive fighters, absolutely without regard for law and order, revengeful, stubborn and when cornered, as desperate as animals.*' [18]

What we are hearing here is the outrage of a white man confronted by blacks who had not been persecuted by whites, who came from multi-racial societies, and who consequently were impertinent enough to believe that they had the right to some civil rights.

The atmosphere of racial tension still prevailed when my father arrived in New York from Howard University in April 1909, his new medical degree in his suitcase – and began to look for work. He quickly became discouraged by what was on offer: work in black hospitals, working only with other black doctors, only on black patients. He had also been thoroughly disillusioned by five years of dealing with racial discrimination in that good old Southern city, Washington. He soon came to the conclusion that there was one simple, obvious solution to his problems: to find work somewhere outside the US.

*

8 The Amazon – And Return To The Caribbean

The first paid job he found as a doctor was not the kind of thing he had in mind, but it appealed to his sense of adventure: he would be a ship's doctor, and not just on any ship.

A crucial factor in the Brazilian rubber boom of the late nineteenth century was the introduction of the Amazonian river steamships; without those steamships, the cities and settlements along the great river could never have developed. The steamships carried freight, they were used as bases for mapping and exploration – and some more surprising functions: many of them were floating brothels. One of the fanciest of them advertised 'frequent sailings to all parts of the river, with champagne on ice and a gramophone all included.' Its erotic services needed no advertising, they were well understood by potential clients. *[19]*

There was a more conventional tourist trade too; luxury steamships that afforded tourists the exciting prospect of living in great comfort, while coming into close contact with the tribal villages, wild life and exotic foliage along the banks of the world's largest river. But there were health risks to these voyages: it was all too easy to contract typhoid, hepatitis or yellow fever. The steamship companies' answer to that problem was to have a doctor on board.

For six hot and steamy months, my father was the ship's doctor, on a boat that sailed between Belem and Manaus, and sometimes ventured further west to give the tourists a safe glimpse of the less developed part of the mighty Amazon. It didn't take him long to decide that he didn't like his job! It was not rewarding medically, his own health, just like that of the passengers, was at risk, and he soon tired of endlessly living on a boat – and decided that he'd prefer to be in a healthier environment on solid ground.

The British *Federal Colony of the Windward Islands* was a group of islands administered by a Governor based in Grenada, and consisted of St. Vincent, St.Lucia, the Grenadines and Barbados. The newly qualified Doctor Megahy wrote to the British administrators and obtained a two-year contract as a Government Medical Officer in St Vincent and St Lucia. The pay wasn't great, but since he had to move between two islands and couldn't establish a permanent residence, his accommodation and subsistence were covered by his employers.

En route to his new job, he stopped in his home country, Barbados. He had been away for five years, and would have noticed many of the things that the former Barbadian, David Straker had noticed on a visit to the Caribbean. Straker described how much the capital city, Bridgetown, had changed since he had left in 1880: *'The rugged ill paved streets were replaced by a macadamized road of pure white stone, which on account of its whiteness, pained the eye of the stranger. Unoccupied spots of land then known to me were now occupied by houses and no unoccupied spot was now to be seen for miles. [20]*

Stores were of greater size and modernity and having a larger stock than of old, much of which I found to be products of the United States. The telegraph, telephone, gas light, tram, railway steam cars – all industries entirely unknown when I left the island are now to be found.

A magnificent set of public buildings across from Trafalgar Square had been erected in which most of the public offices are located.

The tram railway cars... ...are drawn by mules driven by colored men. The conductors are all colored men. The steam railway extends from Fairchild street in Bridgetown to St Andrews, a distance of about thirty miles. The coaches are very ordinary and will accommodate about forty two persons. The freight cars are laden with sugar chiefly and other goods.

There is one theater called the Wilhelmina situated on High Street. This is the only place of its kind in the island and will seat about one thousand persons. A large, possibly the largest structure in the island save the public buildings, is the Barbados Mutual Life Insurance Building situated at the foot of Lower Broad Street. It is a magnificent structure of three stories high.' [21]

Bridgetown certainly wasn't a metropolis, but it was a city where my father could have lived a very pleasant and untroubled life. St Lucia, where my father would spend most of the next two years of his life, could hardly have been more different.

*

Lippincott's Gazetteer described St Lucia in 1906 as *'of a volcanic nature with rugged and largely precipitous slopes. The greater part of the island is covered with dense forests, but the valleys and lower slopes are well cultivated and remarkably productive. Staple products are Sugar, rum, logwood, spices and cacao. Formerly, a staple had been coffee. There is also a sulphur mine.'*

Doesn't sound like a lot of fun, does it?

When my father arrived there, the population was something under 60,000, and over 90% were former slaves of African origin. It was a coaling station for British ships, but there were few roads, and the island was generally quite primitive. Straker observed that the capital, Castries, was *'a small and rather ancient-looking spot. Little or no activity is seen among the people in general, but they are a clever and polite class... Little valley or plain is found, so the town rises suddenly along the side of the hills and mountains, along which may be seen the residences of most of the inhabitants. Travel is performed mostly on horseback or with donkeys, which are used as beast of burden. Women are to be seen as laborers, carrying coal for the numerous steamers which enter here for coal.... ...The white people in St Lucia are few.'*

After Chicago and New York – and even Barbados with its theatre and small railroad – St.Lucia was almost as great a shock to my father as stepping off the *Etruria* on to Ellis Island. Much of his work would be done at the hospital, which was then twenty years old. But he also had to make regular trips into the hinterland, long solitary horseback rides to reach some of his more remote patients. Due to the mountainous nature of the island, it was actually easier to access some areas by traveling around the coast by boat.

Although he spent most of his time in St Lucia, he also had to visit and care for patients in St Vincent, which was, if anything, even more primitive.

Both islands had been French colonies, and most of

the inhabitants spoke only a French patois, which is still spoken by many of them. In fact, the only reason that I know that my father worked in the islands is due to the fact that French was spoken there.

In 1959 I went to the South of France for a holiday, and in St Tropez, I met a very attractive young woman from Paris, Marie Claude, whose parents had a villa along the coast, east of Cannes, at Cap d'Antibes. After a few days in St Tropez, she returned to Cap d'Antibes, and a few days later, I followed her.

Marie Claude introduced me to the trendy villages of St Paul de Vence and Haut de Cagnes, to La Garoupe, the beach at Cap d'Antibes where Scott and Zelda Fitzgerald had summered in the 1920's, and to nightclubs in Monte Carlo and Cannes. I remember there was a new club in Cannes called the Whisky a Gogo and when I asked what sort of a band it had, she told me it played records over a powerful sound system. 'Records?' I said. 'That'll never catch on!'

In the winding streets above La Garoupe, Marie Claude's parents had a pleasant villa with a pool. In the couple of weeks I spent there, I became pretty close with her, and we kept in touch when she returned to Paris and I returned to London.

A few weeks later, she called me and told me that her 16 year old sister was visiting London for a few days, and asked if I would look after her. Naturally, I agreed, and spent some time with the young girl, and took her to my parents' home in Chigwell, Essex, a village on the edge of London, for dinner one evening. Marie Claude's sister spoke little English, and I introduced her to my mother, translating as I went along. But when I introduced her to my father, he startled me by speaking to her in excellent French.

'I didn't know you could speak French,' I said.

He shrugged, 'I had to learn French when I was a young man.'

'At school?'

He shook his head, 'No, for my work.'

He seemed reluctant to continue, but I asked why he had to learn French for his work.

'For a while,' he said, 'I had a job as a Government Medical Officer in the Windward Islands, in St Lucia and St Vincent. They were French colonies before Britain took them over, the people still spoke French, and I found that if I wanted to communicate with my patients, to understand the symptoms they described, I had to learn the language.'

He laughed. 'It's been so long that I'm surprised that I've remembered as much as I have this evening!'

Later, he told me that in St Lucia he had also learned to ride a horse, to get around and see his patients. It was one of the few occasions when my father disclosed any details about his early life, and he probably regretted revealing himself even as little as he had by speaking to Marie Claude's sister in her own language. But that incident was the only reason that I knew of his sojourn in the Windward Islands, a piece of knowledge that was to be highly significant when I began to investigate his life so many years later.

Working in St Lucia and St Vincent was a steep learning curve for my father; at the time he was only twenty-five. If, after a couple of hour's ride to a remote village on a horse, he found a puzzling case, there was no medical back-up, no telephone, nobody else to consult. As well as French, he had to learn to be medically self-sufficient – and he learned something very important about himself: he had a natural instinct for diagnosis.

The need to improvise, to find creative solutions, made the work satisfying, but when he wasn't working, there was very little to do in St.Lucia. It's not surprising that he sought to amuse himself with the company of island girls, and it's easy to imagine the young Doctor Megahy catching their eye. He was educated, he had traveled, and his noted charm only enhanced his natural good looks. No doubt he had his choice of female companions, and in the easy-going style of the islands, his light skin would have meant that young women of any race were within his reach.

*

The one novelty for my father, after his American experience, was that in the islands, he treated white patients. Nevertheless, he was glad when his government contract came to an end, and he was able to return to the comparatively metropolitan life of Bridgetown. There, he stayed with old friends and had time to think about what he wanted to do with his life.

He was considering staying in Barbados, building a life and a career there. He joined a local Masonic Lodge, an ideal springboard for starting his own medical practice, but during his sojourn in St Vincent and St Lucia, his parents had remained on 99th Street in New York. He also knew by now, with his experience of Chicago and New York, even with all their problems, that he was a person who loved and needed the variety of life in a big city.

He had his Howard degree and he could simply have returned to the US, to all the sophistication that the developed world had to offer, but as an 'African Colored', he would still be a second class citizen there. He wondered how he could ever adjust to that.

Finally, he came up with a new strategy. Because his living expenses had been paid in the islands, he had been able to save most of his salary, and now he had the funds to return to the US with a plan to beat the bigotry he had faced previously. He returned to the US with a new determination.

*

9 Back to New York – 'Passing' Fails

My father's plan was to get a second medical degree, this time from a university that had no race connotations. He felt that with his pale skin, and his straight hair, he had a good chance of 'passing' as white, and that the only thing that had branded him beyond doubt as a black man was his degree from Howard. His parents thought he was crazy, and when he told his brother Evan in Chicago what he was going to do, they got into a furious argument. Evan believed that he should make the best of his life as himself, not by pretending to be someone else.

But my father's mind was made up: he was not going to live a life of deference to whites. With the savings from his British government job, he was able to pay his fees at New York University, and with the experience he already had, he was able to negotiate merely attending a short refresher course there. It was no surprise when he passed the examinations in October 1912 with exceptionally high marks. But again, like Howard, he formed no friendships with any other student.

Meanwhile, he was trying out his new white identity in New York. As long as he kept out of colored areas, he was able to pass. If he was asked about his origins, he learned to say that he was Greek or Turkish. Black Africa never seemed to occur to his questioners. He was discovering that he had a talent for inventing stories about his life.

A year after he got back from Barbados, with his new qualifications from NYU, he was ready to put his plan to the real test: finding work. He was in for a disappointment; it quickly became apparent that even his new NYU degree didn't liberate him from the clutches of racism.

Fatefully, he had already been listed by the American Medical Association with his Howard degree, which was enough for them to identifying him forever as black and deny his request for membership. The AMA refused to change that listing, so not only was he barred from joining the Association itself, but any hospital or potential employer or patient who checked him out could immediately discover that however white the man in front of them might look – white he was not.

He could only work in black hospitals, or substitute for black doctors who were sick or on vacation. He never managed to treat white patients, and in his daily life he still ran into white Americans who called him 'boy'.

Black doctors retaliated against the AMA by forming their own associations, but the AMA refused to recognize those associations, and continued to list the race of doctors well into the 1960's. It took almost one hundred years after my father graduated from Howard, for the AMA to issue this statement in July 2008:

The American Medical Association officially apologizes for its history of excluding black physicians from membership, for listing black doctors as 'colored' in its National Physician Directory for decades, and for failing to speak against federal funding of segregated hospitals and in favor of civil rights legislation.[22]

So it wasn't surprising that back in 1913, my father

found it difficult to get work. But my grandparents were still living in their house on West 99th Street, a pretty good neighborhood. After some discussion with his family, they agreed that he could set up his own practice – in their house. He joined the Medical Society of New York, which did not delve into the racial background of its members, but nevertheless he didn't use his Howard degree, but his qualifications from NYU.

When I saw his professional listing in the Society's archives, it made his life in New York real for me for the first time. It was an eerie feeling finding his office hours and a phone number I could have called to get an appointment with the young Dr Megahy:

Megahy, James Kenneth Campbell
Phone number: Circle 2937
Address: 15, W.99th Street
Office hours: 8 till 11, 6 to 8

*

For reasons I'll never know, his practice failed. Of course, he was operating in a white neighborhood, and perhaps once more racism was the problem. It may have been something else, but the tide was running against black people, and America was trending not away from racism, but back toward it. In 1913, the noose of racism was tightened a little further with the election of President Woodrow Wilson.

At Wilson's Inauguration, Washington rang with happy Rebel Yells, bands all over town played *Dixie*, and the new President was sworn in by the Chief Justice of the Supreme Court – who was a former member of the Ku Klux Klan. According to historian

Lawrence J Friedman *[23]*, 'an unidentified associate of the new Chief Executive warned that since the South now ran the nation, Negroes should expect to be treated as a servile race.'

Wilson's racism was not clandestine. The voters who put him in office knew that when he was previously President of Princeton, he had turned away black applicants, regarding their desire for university education as 'unwarranted.'

In a bizarre distortion of the reality of Wilson's views, the adjective 'Wilsonian' has come to suggest a positive and idealistic vision for the extension of justice and democratic values throughout the world. In a speech to the Senate in 1917, he did say, '*No nation should seek to extend its polity over any other nation or people...every nation should be left free to determine its own policy, the little along with the great and powerful.*'

This was the statement establishing his 'doctrine of self-determination', but when it came to the black population of his own country, this unrepentant racist's only determination was that they would be subservient to the whites.

As soon as he took office, he set about doing all he could to shrink the meager civil and democratic rights that were left to blacks after the depredations of Redemption.

In the Washington that my father knew while he was at Howard, Reconstruction had brought access to federal jobs for the city's large black population, who worked with whites in virtually integrated conditions. Wilson's cabinet quickly stopped all that, re-introducing segregation of the toilets, cafeterias, and work areas of government departments. Most black diplomats were replaced by whites; many black federal officials were removed; the Washington Police and Fire Department stopped hiring blacks.

In a press conference in the White House, Wilson told a group of reporters that 'segregation is not a humiliation, but a benefit'. When one journalist, William Monroe Trotter, challenged that assertion, Wilson told him abruptly, 'Your manner offends me!' and asked him to leave the building.

This institutionalized racism, from the very heights of government, affected the atmosphere everywhere in the US, including New York and Chicago.

My father would also certainly have known about, if not seen, the openly racist, Klan-praising movie, D.W. Griffith's *The Birth of a Nation*, which was released in 1915. Its original title was The Klansman. Based on a novel by one Thomas Dixon, a close friend of Woodrow Wilson, the movie described how heroic white men overthrew blacks (portrayed in the movie by white actors in blackface makeup) who had risen above their merited station in life through what was described as the 'folly of Reconstruction'.

It was not only screened for Congress and the Supreme Court, but when it was shown to the Cabinet, it became the first film to be shown in the White House. In theaters, it was a huge hit. Not a proud moment for the country, and this whole episode was full of disturbing resonances for my father.

He continued to visit his brother Evan in Chicago, sometimes getting work there as a replacement doctor for a week or two. What he saw in Chicago of the life of blacks, in one of the more tolerant cities in the nation, finally convinced him that if he truly wanted to change his life, he had to change his location.

In 1914, he hit on the idea that one of the easiest opportunities open to him was to practice medicine in Canada. He was, after all, born in a British Colony, so he would have no trouble going to Canada and working there. He had visited Canada and liked the country, and knew that slavery and racism against blacks had never been a factor in Canadian life.

Even before slavery's abolition by the British Empire, the slave population in Canada never numbered more than 5,000, mostly domestic servants. This wasn't because the Canadians were idealistic and opposed to racism, it was because the Canadian economy was not based on plantation agriculture and had no need of a slave labor force. By 1834, when slavery was abolished throughout the British Empire, there were probably fewer than 50 slaves in the country [24]; and Canada was the ultimate destination of many escaped slaves along the legendary Underground Railroad.

So in November, 1914, my father went to Halifax, to Dalhousie Medical School, to take the preliminary examination of the Medical Board of the Province of Nova Scotia. He passed the entrance examination, of course, but in the weeks afterwards had to face the fact that there was one aspect of Canadian life that he found deeply unpalatable: the bitterly cold winters. The short dark days, the snow and ice, were not to the taste of a man accustomed to swimming year round in the warm waters around Barbados; he decided to look elsewhere.

He had always kept in touch with with his half-brother Norman Brewster, who was by this time established as a doctor in Port of Spain, Trinidad. There was no international telephone, but they regularly exchanged letters.

My father was especially interested in Norman's experiences at medical school in Britain. Norman, much darker skinned, and clearly of African descent, had experienced no hostility or racism there. According to Norman, race was a far less important matter in Britain than in the US. In fact, Norman enthusiastically recommended his own alma mater, Edinburgh University.

My father had lived with his parents on 99th Street during and after his time at NYU, and once again, he had saved his money. He could afford to pay his fare to Scotland, and his tuition. He discovered that Edinburgh Medical School would give him some credit for his Howard and NYU degrees, and that he could get a degree there after only a couple of years.

My father had tremendous energy, quiet but relentless persistence, and by now he knew that he was a risk-taker. He was also more determined than ever not to have his life defined by racism. If it meant leaving the US, so be it.

*

10 Scotland, England – and Canada

It's difficult to know just how specific was my father's knowledge of race relations in Britain; all of his information would have come from his half-brother, who had apparently enjoyed his time at Edinburgh University. The medical school there was considered to be one of the best in Europe, and counted among its illustrious alumni no less than Charles Darwin.

After he qualified, Norman had returned to live in the Caribbean, but my father was taking a much bolder decision: he was planning a permanent move to Britain. His boat docked in Liverpool on December 17th 1916.

In 1899 when Norman was a student at the Edinburgh medical school, there were more than two hundred other students from the British colonies studying there, but over the next two decades, due to competition from Oxford and Cambridge, which offered residential facilities, their numbers declined. There had been talk of establishing a residence for foreign students, but it didn't happen, and my father found lodgings at 16, Panmuir Place, less than half a mile from the University.

Almost a hundred years later, when I went to see 16, Panmuir Place, it was still a student lodging house.

When my father enrolled on the Edinburgh campus, he slowly realized that his fellow students from India and other British colonies would be among the few dark-skinned people he would meet in Britain. In spite of Britain's historical role in the slave trade, dark faces were still very rare on British streets.

The few black people in Britain were mostly sailors who had jumped ship or descendants of slaves imported from West Africa as domestic servants in the eighteenth century. British slavery was always an overseas program – the slaves were never needed to work in Britain, but in the British Empire.

But in 1772, the celebrated Somersett case virtually outlawed slavery in Britain long before its formal abolition. Charles Stewart, a visiting Customs officer from Boston, Massachusetts, had brought his slave James Somersett with him to London. When Somersett escaped, Stewart recaptured him and locked him up on a ship bound for Jamaica.

But three English people claiming to be Somersett's Godparents, got him released with a writ of Habeas Corpus, pending a trial to determine his legal status.

Somersett's lawyer claimed that slavery might be legal in the Colonies, but no English law or Statute permitted it in Britain. The Chief Justice, Lord Mansfield, concurred, saying that, *'The state of slavery is of such a nature, that it is incapable of being introduced on any reason, moral or political; but only positive law, which preserves its force long after the reasons, occasion, and time itself from whence it was created, is erased from memory: it's so odious, that nothing can be suffered to support it, but positive law. Whatever inconveniences, therefore, may follow from a decision, I cannot say this case is allowed or approved by the law of England; and therefore the black must be discharged.' [24]*

It was 23rd June 1772, a day that was later widely regarded as 'the End of Slavery'...well, not quite, but Lord Mansfield's judgement was of immense symbolic power.

Uncharitably, one might say that the main reason that English people had no strong feelings about black Africans was simply because there were virtually none in the British Isles; but they also had no history of conflict and competition with black nations, so they never developed the disdain for them that they felt for the French or the Germans or 'foreigners' in general. Whatever the reasons, a black person could live freely in Britain in a way unknown in the US.

The celebrated black author and anti-slavery activist, Frederick Douglass, spent two years in Britain in the nineteenth century, and nobody has written better of their feelings of escaping from the clutches of racism. In an echo of the famous Shylock speech in *The Merchant of Venice,* he wrote, *'I breathe, and lo! The chattel becomes a man! I gaze around in vain for one who will question my equal humanity, claim me as a slave, or offer me an insult. I employ a cab - I am seated beside white people - I am shown into the same parlor - I dine at the same table - and no one is offended. No delicate nose grows deformed in my presence.*

I find no difficulty here in obtaining admission into any place of worship, instruction, or amusement, on equal terms with people as white as any I ever saw in the United States. I meet nothing to remind me of my complexion. I find myself regarded and treated at every turn with kindness and deference paid to white people. When I go to church I am met by no upturned nose and scornful lip, to tell me, 'We don't allow niggers in here!' [25]

My father also met nothing to 'remind him of his

complexion' on arriving in Britain.

He was now thirty-one years old, and had endured more than a decade of constant appraisal of his race. His feelings of relief and release at being in a country where his skin color and features were of no account must have been as strong as to Douglass's.

Of course, it wasn't that the British were more open-minded or less bigoted than their cousins and descendants in the US. In the early twentieth century, when my father got to Edinburgh, the population of Britain had grown to thirty-five million, but the black minority was still tiny, not more than 25,000. They were concentrated in port cities like London, Bristol and Liverpool, where their numbers were so small that there was no friction caused by competition with the whites for jobs or housing.

For the most part, relations between blacks and whites were peaceful to an extent hardly imaginable in the US. The one moment of trouble between the races came when the the First World War ended in 1918 and thousands of former soldiers returned to the country, expecting to find a 'Land Fit For Heroes'. Instead, they found unemployment, poverty – and a few black immigrants marrying white British girls.

The weather is always a factor in riots, and in the blistering heat of the summer of 1919, the ex-soldiers' anger and dissatisfaction in their first summer back in Britain, turned to violence. Race riots broke out in the dock areas of London, Liverpool and Cardiff. In London, where there were hardly any blacks to have a riot with, the rioters focused on the small Chinese community.

In those three British cities two men lost their lives,

a number of others were beaten and some fires were started, but these riots were very tame by comparison with those in the US. No riots were reported in Edinburgh, or generally in Scotland, where there were no ethnic people of any kind.

*

On the official entry forms to the Edinburgh Medical School, my father entered his place of birth correctly as 'Barbados BWI' – British West Indies. This would be the very last time he would ever tell the truth about that. With his degrees from Howard and NYU, and his practical experience as a doctor, he was a spectacularly successful student, and in two and a half years years, he graduated from Edinburgh, on July 19th 1918.

Edinburgh might have been my father's opportunity to forge friendships with other students, but I never heard him speak of any friends he made there. Whatever his social life as a student in Scotland was, he kept it to himself.

On my mother's side of the family, family lore about my father – which is a nice way of saying 'the story he chose to tell them' – was that he had come from Canada with the motive of furthering his medical education with a degree from one of the best medical schools in Europe. That may not have been his primary motive, but he was duly inaugurated as a Fellow of both the Royal College of Physicians and the Royal College of Surgeons, so that he could put the prized initials FRCP, FRCS after his name.

When he left Scotland, he plan did seem to have

worked and he apparently felt able to express himself more freely and develop a new, 'white' persona. He wasn't flamboyant, but he no longer felt pressured to keep a low profile. He had already developed his fascination with cars and when I once asked him about the first cars he had owned, he told me that his first car in Britain was an Austin Doctor's Coupe.

I had never heard of a 'Doctor's Coupe' and he explained that in the US, the first mass-produced car, the Model T Ford, was a big hit with doctors in remote areas of the country. They bought the 2-door coupe in large numbers, they were mostly single men who only needed two seats, and they welcomed the large trunk in which they could carry all the medical equipment a rural doctor might need. People began calling these Model T's 'Doctor's Coupes'. Other manufacturers quickly seized on this market and by the 1920's, Dodge, Lincoln, Buick and Studebaker all made Doctor's Coupes; in England Austin made one – as did Rolls Royce.

My father's Austin Doctor's Coupe was a used car, and he didn't much like it. So he saved until he could afford something more 'interesting'.

I asked what that was and he said, 'It was a Donnet-Zedel.'

'A what?' I'd never heard of it.

He told me that it was a French car, which was only made for a few years. Decades later, I found a photograph of that Donnet-Zedel model on the internet: it was a rakish four-seater convertible, with a bold brass radiator and stylishly swept front wings. Not exactly a 'doctor's car', but by then my father was more confident about being himself. [26]

His professional career in Britain began with a series of jobs working as a locum, the English term for a substitute doctor, derived from the Latin, *Locum Tenens*, holding the place of.

The locum's accommodation was always provided by the doctor who had hired him, so once more he was able to save money, and in three years had enough to buy a small medical practice in St.Neots, in Cambridgeshire. St.Neots, a charming old market town dating back to the Roman occupation of Britain, is about 50 miles from London and less than 30 miles from Cambridge.

Things went well for my father in St.Neots until one day in early 1924, while he was out making house calls – which he continued to do right up to the day he died – and his own house caught fire and burned down, for reasons unknown. Worse, he had not kept up his property insurance. In the ensuing financial chaos, he lost his ownership of the house, had to sell his much-prized Donnet-Zedel, and had to start his working life all over again, beginning once more as a locum.

Now, he worked all over the country, going wherever jobs were available, until one of those locum jobs, in the office of a Doctor Edward Hirson, took him to Manchester, a city that would be the location of another turning point in his life.

So that was our family version of the beginning of my father's life in Britain. In looking at how much of that narrative was true, I had to remember that this was a man who instinctively had the tradecraft of a spy; all his mythical stories about his life rubbed against the truth here and there. He did indeed live in St.Neots, and he probably did own a Donnet-Zedel. His distortions took the form of omissions and when I was making a routine check of transatlantic ships' manifests of their passengers, to get an exact date of his arrival in Britain in the winter of 1916, I stumbled on a very significant one: on my computer screen I saw records of other voyages of which I had never heard anything.

I was astonished to find that he had returned to North America in 1924, on a boat that docked in Halifax, Nova Scotia, a city he knew well from when he had taken the Dalhousie entrance examination there ten years before. Fortunately, Canadian Immigration documents, like those of Ellis Island, have been computerized. When I looked at the information my father had filled in on his entry forms into Canada, I got more surprises: he had lied about three very significant facts.

He had deducted four years from his age, writing that he was 35; he stated that his place of birth was Carluke, in Scotland; he had not used Kenneth – his first name, by which everyone called him – but simply wrote his first and last names as James Megahy.

Then, yet another new entry appeared on my screen: his date of return to Britain. This was in September 1930, the year he met my mother.

This was a very different chronology from the story he had told my mother and her family, which was that after getting his degree from Edinburgh, he had remained in Britain, right up until he met my mother. Like the rest of my family, I had never heard of his sojourn in Canada, and I became very curious about that missing period in his life, the six years from 1924 to 1930.

I had a pretty good idea of why he might have left Britain: he had suffered a major setback in the fire, losing his house and all of his possessions; and it was eight years since he had seen his brother Evan. Canada was a form of British Colony, which did not gain its independence from Britain until 1926, and even then, there were still many constitutional ties between the two countries, including the critical fact that Canada recognized British academic qualifications.

It made sense that he would have another try at life in Canada. With one change of trains, most of the major cities in Eastern Canada were only a few hours away from Evan Megahy in Chicago; and in Canada every opportunity open to a white man was available to my father. In that period, as in Britain, racism was virtually non-existent .

But that raises the question of why he had lied on his immigration forms, and the answer is clear. He was determined not to be identified as that 'African Colored' Kenneth Megahy from Barbados with a Howard degree. That objective was easily achieved when his changed name, his changed date and place of birth, were combined with his Edinburgh degree, which entitled him to practice medicine in Canada. He had re-invented himself; now he was the thirty-five year old Dr James Megahy, FRCS, FRCP, Edinburgh. A Scotsman.

In thinking about all this, I recalled two items that had been carried around by my family from my grandmother's house on Thirlmere Street in Manchester, to East Ham in London, to Chingford in Essex, and eventually to Chigwell, Essex. The first was a thick leather-bound book, a history of the Canadian province of Manitoba. I had looked at this book a couple of times as a child and not found it very interesting.

The other item was a small bakelite object, I'm not even sure what it was. It consisted of an oval platform some four inches long. Something had been removed from it so that half the platform was empty, and the other half was taken up with the figure of black-faced minstrel, dancing with a cane. Around the front edge of this object was the inscription, 'Chasing the Blues in Winnipeg 1926'.

Winnipeg is the major city in Manitoba, and although I don't have much doubt that this where my father made his Canadian home, this was another part of his life he never talked about.

I do know that my father and my uncle had decided together about my cousin Robert's education. I always thought that any discussion they had was in correspondence – now I know that those conversations were face to face.

While my father was in Canada, he often visited Evan, and they managed to patch up their differences, mainly by not talking about them. Evan told his brother that he wanted his son to have the best possible education, and this was at least something on which they were in complete agreement. My father suggested that Evan should consider sending Robert to school in Britain. Their cultural heritage from Barbados was heavily slanted towards Britain, and this struck Evan as a good suggestion.

My father apparently learned to tolerate the severe Canadian winters and his life there was pleasant enough, but he was trying to set himself up for the long term. He could not have imagined when he boarded the boat for Halifax that within a very few years, the entire Western world was going to be shaken by a huge crisis, which would engulf the lives of millions of people, and smash all his plans.

The US Wall Street Crash of 1929 and the ensuing Great Depression had a rapid and massive impact on its neighbor to the north. Within three years, industrial production in Canada had fallen to only just over half its 1929 level, gross domestic product had also fallen to just over half its 1929 level, and both levels were the second lowest in the world after the United States itself. Exports of raw materials, prices and profits plunged. In every sector of the economy employment fell.

In 1929, my father would have seen unpleasant changes in Winnipeg: agricultural workers, their lives already ravaged by the ecological disaster of The Dust Bowl in the Great Plains, had begun to flood into Canadian cities, looking for work. He would have seen the same soup kitchens, bread lines and despairing workers as he had seen when visiting Evan in Depression Chicago. Even Evan's medical practice was hit by the Depression, but he was now the Junior City Engineer of Chicago, with that now rare commodity, a reliable pay check.

In the US, my father had only been allowed to work with black patients; in Canada he had not faced that restriction, but now work itself was difficult to find, even for doctors. But as Canada's economy and infrastructure collapsed, my father was one of the lucky ones: he had an escape route. Britain was suffering its own Depression, but on nothing like the scale of North America. In Britain, in the three years after 1929, industrial production only fell by 17%.

My father might have preferred life in North America, but Britain wasn't so bad, the winters were not as ferocious – and he was confident that he could find work there.

Evan encouraged him to return to Britain; there was something in it for Evan too. He had taken the decision to send his son Robert, who had turned out to be perfectly white-skinned, to school in England. Discussing it with my father, they had chosen the prestigious private school, Harrow, the alma mater of no less than Winston Churchill.

This was a spectacular ambition for a man of mixed race in the US in the 1920's, since of English schools, Harrow was then second only to Eton in prestige. The school of course would have no idea that their new white-skinned student was in fact legally black in his home country.

If my father returned to Britain he would be able to keep an eye on his nephew, and Robert could spend the shorter vacations with him.

My father had maintained contact with his friend Dr Hirson in Manchester, and had throughout his absence even continued to pay his subscriptions to the British Medical Association, using Hirson's address. He wrote to Hirson, advising him of his plan to return, and when Hirson wrote back to say that he was planning an extended vacation and needed a locum, that clinched it and my father seized the chance to try his luck in Britain again.

But why did he never talk about this period in his

life?

When he returned to Britain, he was forty-five years old, still a youthful and handsome man, with an olive skin and dark, almost girlish eyes, and people still commented on his good looks. In Canada, did the handsome doctor become involved in a romantic entanglement which had ended badly? I'll never know.

This time he was determined to make a very serious, carefully considered and permanent effort to re-invent himself once more. On September 10th 1930, he set sail from Montreal, direct to the port of Manchester, where the next chapter of his life would start surprisingly soon.

*

11 The Forger

One fine morning in 1930, shortly after returning to Britain, James Kenneth Campbell Megahy, sat at the dining table in the living room of his small, rented house in Regent Road, Salford, a suburb of Manchester. He had just finished his breakfast and the drapes in the room were still drawn from the evening before, so that although it was a sunny day, the room was dark, which felt appropriate to his purpose.

The table top was covered with several pieces of paper with diagrams and notes on them: names, places and dates. He compared information, crossed out some words and added new ones, rearranging the patterns of the pieces of paper. Then finally, he picked up an old, worn Victorian Anglican Bible and opened it to the flyleaf.

He picked up his fountain pen, and starting at the top of the page, began very carefully, in a neat, clear hand, to copy the information from the scattered pages on to the flyleaf.

He wrote the first names and dates:

Nathaniel Forte, born Galway 7th April 1794.
Mary Bilcah Springer born Cork, June 12th 1798
Children:

Sarah Jane Forte born Galway Oct 6th 1822 [my great grandmother]

Robert Sheremiah Megahy [my great grandfather] born Waterford 10th August 1829 son of Jacob Israel Megahy & Ruth Leah Megahy of Cork

Marriage:

Sarah Jane Forte [my great-grandmother] + Robert Sheremiah Megahy 10th February 1854, Waterford

Children:

James Megahy [my grandfather] born Tuarn Co Galway 1st November 1855 Mary Maud Megahy [my grandfather's sister] born Galway 2nd May 1860

He continued on down the century and down the page, until he filled it with his entire family tree. His own entry reads:

James Kenneth Campbell Megahy, born Halifax, Nova Scotia, 19th November 1889.

Underneath it, he wrote:

Migrated to Toronto June 1892

Migrated to Buffalo 1894

Migrated to Panama 1895

Below that, he recorded the deaths of his parents:

Died:

James Megahy April 16th 1919 - Barbados

Died:

Frances Anne Thorne Megahy - March 24th 1923 in New York

He had laid out the history of his entire family for over one hundred years. He checked it and was pleased with his work; he had made no mistakes, nothing needed correcting or erasing. He made sure that the ink was dry, replaced the screw top on his pen, walked to the window and pulled back the curtain. Now the sun streamed in, onto the table top. He placed the open Bible in a shaft of sunlight. Soon, the ink would be faded, and the family tree would look to the casual eye as if it was written years before. He checked his watch: his first patient would soon arrive. He stood up and left the room.

Interestingly, among this false information, he had given away his knowledge of his true ancestry when he invented the name 'Nathaniel Forte'; his grandmother's maiden name was Forte, taken from the slave who was her father.

But the truth of this family tree didn't matter to him; at this stage in his life, his sense of reality was merely a collection of experiences and memories that he could spin into any personal narrative that he needed. He could draw on his several years of experience of life in Canada, his accent had mellowed in the quarter of a century since he had left the Caribbean.

In an extraordinary switch, he no longer needed to be James Megahy, the Scottish doctor: he was now completely confident in his ability to present himself to the world as a Canadian Doctor, this time of Irish descent.

*

12 Refuge – In A Ghetto

It was in the 1960's that I became conscious of black Americans using the word ghetto, a word I felt that they had slipped out from under the Jews' noses without anyone noticing. There was a song at that time, *In the Ghetto*, which amused me because I had long, long before that become accustomed to the idea that my own life had started in a ghetto, and a thoroughly Jewish one at that.

It was my fate to be born in the ghetto; but my father became part of it by choice – a choice that again entwined his life with race and bigotry.

To understand my father's decision, you have to understand the family he married into in the north of England, the family that became the basis for his entire life in Britain from his mid-forties onwards, the family indeed which served as an essential part of his lifelong 'cover': the Cohens of Manchester.

Dr Hirson's medical office, where my father worked for a few critical weeks in the fall of 1930, was in the working class district of Hightown in Manchester, which had been built for the new army of textile workers who drifted in from the fields in the Industrial Revolution — rows of small two story brick houses, lining narrow, cobbled streets, a couple of miles from the city center. In the late nineteenth century, as those early textile workers became more prosperous and moved on, their place was taken by a wave of Jewish immigrants from Eastern Europe, principally from Russia.

When the Czar Alexander 11 was assassinated by 'anarchists' in Moscow in 1881, the impoverished

Russian peasantry was easily persuaded of the fiction that he was the victim of a Jewish plot, and went on a rampage all over Southern Russia, massacring Jews, raping their women and burning down their houses. The result was a massive migration, mostly to the United States, but a significant number of Russian Jews came to England, and many of them found their way to Manchester, where their number jumped from 5,000 in 1880 to 30,000 in 1890 *[27]*.

The Manchester Jews' folklore of persecution was not only about the Czar's *pogroms*; by the time my father arrived in Manchester, they had added to it the irrational anti-Semitic outrages committed during the First World War. In a horrible irony, revealed by our foresight into the Holocaust to come, the Jews' names were perceived by the ignorant working class gentile citizens of Manchester as German – so their businesses were burned, their shop windows broken, their children taunted.

Manchester had been the first city in the world to take advantage of the invention of new weaving techniques, and it quickly became the dominant world center of cotton goods production. The Jewish immigrants arriving there in the 1880's found themselves in a very wealthy city, nicknamed variously 'Cottonopolis' and 'The Capital of Cotton'.

But where did the cotton come from, and who picked it? Originally, Manchester's prosperity was based on raw cotton imported from the colonial slave plantations via the port of Liverpool and then along the Manchester Ship Canal to the area's textile mills and cotton warehouses. The city of Manchester was a key link in an industry that depended on slave labor in the US for its raw material.

During the War Between the States, part of the pressure put on the South by the North was a Union naval blockade of cotton exports from the Confederacy to northern England, in an attempt to cut off a vital source of war-time finance. Ironically, this city with its intimate and historical dependency on slavery, was the city that my father, the descendant of slaves, chose to settle in.

In my childish recollection, the few Hightown streets that comprised the Jewish ghetto seemed like a vast area, and indeed they probably were so perceived by their adult Jewish inhabitants, whose mental horizons hardly stretched beyond Hightown.

When my father walked through the streets of Hightown in 1930, he stepped back in time to a world little removed from the East European *stetls* my Jewish grandparents had fled from forty years before.

All Jewish village life could be found there. The *schul*, for worship, for a *bris*, a barmitzvah, a wedding or a funeral; Black's Deli for kosher food — my cousin Alma married the Blacks' son, Abie; Bookbinders the bakery for *kugel*; and there were tailors, watchmakers, shoemakers, everything you needed to avoid to giving business to the dreaded *goyim*. On the face of it, this was a most unlikely environment for my father to swear allegiance to, but that is precisely what happened.

Avram Cohen, my mother's father, had arrived in England from Odessa in the 1880's, bizarrely enough escaping a Russian Army recruiting campaign, although what they would have done with this short Jewish neophyte I can't imagine. If the recruiters had captured him, he would have faced no less than 25 years as a conscript, so he was highly motivated to escape their clutches.

'He jumped into the river and swam across!' my mother would cry excitedly, telling the story, 'with the Czar's men shooting at him. With bullets, Francis!'

If only I had some similar stories from my father's side of the family...

My grandmother had arrived earlier than her husband-to-be. In 1874, she was only fourteen when she made the complex and hazardous trans-European journey from her village in Lithuania by train, completely alone, with Russian and Yiddish her only languages – a daunting initiative test for a teenage girl in that era. Her strategy was to make herself look as old as possible.

She was supposed to meet her brother, whom she had not seen since she was seven years old, on the docks in Hull, when her boat landed. Although a number of men eyed the pretty young blonde, her brother was nowhere to be found. However, she had enough money for a train ticket to Manchester, and a piece of paper with the address of a boarding house there; she had got this far, and was not to be daunted now. She bought a ticket and boarded the train, one of those divided into compartments, with no linking corridor.

A moment later, just before the train chugged out of the station, a man stepped into the compartment. He was bearded, dark-eyed, and to her horror, she recalled that he had been amongst the men checking her out on the dockside. She looked out of the window, and each time the train went through a tunnel, drew back fearfully in her seat.

But the train reached Manchester without the man assaulting her, or even addressing a single word to her. Indeed, he leaped off the train and walked away rapidly as soon as it stopped. With a sigh of relief, the young girl found a hansom cab, handed the driver her piece of paper, and some twenty minutes later she was welcomed into a Jewish boarding house by a friendly, older woman, who spoke Yiddish. She showed the girl into a parlor and went to get her room ready.

A few moments later, the door opened, and the fourteen year old's heart almost stopped: there stood the sinister man from the train.

Then he smiled broadly, opened his arms and greeted her in Yiddish. It was her brother. They had not seen each other for so long and had both changed so much, that earlier in the day they had simply not recognized each other.

By the time of my father's encounter with the Manchester Jews, even before the undreamed-of horrors of the Holocaust, he found a community that was fearful and inward-looking, deeply suspicious of their xenophobic British hosts: apprehensions he found strikingly similar to those of the black communities he knew in Washington, Chicago and New York. To some extent those apprehensions had been fueled, and even justified, by those attacks made on Jewish businesses during the First World War.

Commensurately, the immense military and industrial power of the Empire had bolstered Britons' suspicions of and contempt for all foreigners. Britain, unlike those derided countries across the Channel, was a clearly defined physical entity: the ocean marked out its borders with a clarity and a permanence unknown in Continental Europe. Foreigners were all assigned — and still have — derogatory nicknames: Krauts for the Germans, Frogs for the French, Eyeties for the Italians, Wogs for anyone from the Colonies, Micks or Paddies for the Irish, Taffies for the Welsh, Jocks for the Scots and Yids or Sheenies for the Jews.

My father recognized the Cohen family's self-image as the regulation one of a persecuted minority, and their self-segregation was buttressed by their iron-clad determination not to be assimilated into British society. On the face of it, the Cohens' eventual acceptance of my father may seem as strange as his decision to throw in his lot with this self-obsessed minority.

Unlike them, he was a man of wide horizons; he had degrees from three different universities, was well traveled and well read. But the paradox was that within their community, with all its paranoia, he was to find a safe haven, because there at least he would never be a solitary target for suspicion.

My mother, Sarah – always known as Sadie – was born in Hightown in 1899, and for the rest of her long life – she died in 1991 – her automatic response on hearing of someone she didn't know, was to ask first if they were Jewish, and then if they came from Manchester. If the answer was positive, i.e. yes on both counts, she would instantly perceive some small bond with them, and almost certainly recall a close relative of theirs with an anecdote. These anecdotes often involved money, how so-and-so's son was a *goniff*, 'He stole from his own family, Francis!' Or he was simply a bad person who had 'knocked' his own brother: got a loan he never intended to pay back.

Sadie Cohen was the youngest of eight children. Her oldest brother, Gabe, had given his life for his country in the trenches of the Somme battlefield in the First World War. Her remaining brothers, Solly, Barney, Jack, and Israel, were all married, as were her two older sisters, Esther and Kath.

When Sadie met my father she was thirty-one years old – and single.

In that era, when the life expectancy of a woman was around fifty-five, she had already lived more than half her life, and to be unmarried in that community at her age was to be virtually without hope of marriage. The pool of Jewish suitors in Manchester was necessarily small, and because of that, Sadie 'knew everybody', so that by the time she was in her late twenties, her only chance of meeting someone new would have been an encounter with an outsider, perhaps from the smaller Jewish community of Leeds, or by some remote chance, from London. Slim pickings indeed, and she had all but given up hope of ever being married, and was, in the slang of the period, 'on the shelf'.

She had made a half-hearted attempt to be a singer and dancer, and although she had neither the stomach nor the talent for the music hall theaters and audiences of the day, she kept alive her dreams of wider horizons.

Sadie could be a difficult character; she was opinionated and outspoken enough to dominate a group – or to intimidate most men. But she was flirtatious, amusing and attractive, so over the years she had received a number of offers of marriage, but none of them had matched her aspirations. She knew there was a sophisticated life beyond Manchester, she had seen glimpses of it at the Tea Dances in the Midland Hotel; she knew that even beyond that, there were the bright lights of London, and she had also heard her older brother Solly talk of his adventures in Canada and the US.

Sadie's mother, my grandmother, was by then in her late sixties and the cataracts that would eventually render her completely blind were at an advanced stage. Someone had to look after her, and who better, reasoned The Family, than her spinster daughter. So Sadie lived in her mother's two-story three-up, three-down family house at 16, Thirlmere Street, one of the larger houses on that ghetto street, where her oldest brothers paid all the expenses and also gave her some money for herself. It was hardly a fulfilling life for the lively and rebellious young woman.

Sadie didn't do the menial household chores; there was a maid for that, Mary, from a community one rung lower on the social ladder in Jewish eyes: the Irish. Another ironic resonance with my father's ancestry. No Jewish family in Hightown had any domestic help from within their own community; those jobs were considered unsuitable for Jews.

Later in her life, when my mother returned from her first visit to Israel, she told me excitedly, 'Even the garbage men are Jewish there, Francis!'

The English host community may have had contempt for these short, dark-eyed immigrants, but if anything, the Jews' contempt for *goys* was greater.

Sadie's old, blind mother was fervently religious, and so every Friday evening and Saturday morning in the winter, Mary would come to the house and make the coal fires that heated it, work that was forbidden to Jews under the strict Sabbath rules observed by my grandmother.

*

A few weeks after my father returned from Canada and was working as Hirson's locum, pure chance transformed his life. My grandmother needed regular medication and my aunt Esther, only a year older than my mother and frequently mistaken for her, lived near to Hirson's office, and always picked up that medication.

But one fateful spring day in 1930, Esther was unable to pick up my grandmother's prescription and asked Sadie to pick it up. When my father opened his office door, he at first thought that Sadie was Esther, and they laughed over his mistake. It was to be the beginning of a great deal of laughter in my father's life.

*

13 Romance

When Sadie was shown into the doctor's office, she was astonished to meet not the old family doctor, but a tan, handsome man with an American accent, who looked a good deal younger than his forty-five years. He would later tell her that he was Canadian-born, and had medical degrees from New York and Edinburgh universities, and had decided to settle in England.

My father was of medium height, with wavy brown hair, which he kept short and parted on the left all his life. His regular features, beautiful dark brown eyes, full lips and straight nose, all gave him a romantic, almost girlish look. He had a slightly rolling gait when he walked, and even when he moved quickly, he had a quality of physical relaxation. He had immense charm, behind which he concealed a surprisingly stubborn and determined nature. His entire manner was relaxed and confident, particularly when he was dealing with patients, and he wore a stillness about him that meant that in a group you might not notice him, but if you did, you would become aware that he had a certain presence.

And who did my father meet? Sadie was a slim but voluptuous woman with dark hair and sparkling blue eyes, and a contagious firecracker energy.

In an instant, both their lives were changed. My mother immediately decided that from now on, she would be picking up her mother's prescription! She had met the glamorous man she had dreamed of, a man who had lived other lives in other countries, an educated man, a man with considerable and steady earning power in those Depression days, a man who could turn those merely imagined horizons of hers into reality. My father knew instinctively that here was a woman who could hold his interest and easily match him in force of personality. She wasn't a patient, was merely collecting a prescription, so he felt that there was no impropriety about asking her to meet him again.

A romance quickly developed between the handsome doctor and the vivacious dark-haired Jewish woman. They complemented each other well. He admired her gregarious nature, so different from his own, and she admired his reflective cast of mind, so different from hers. In sheer intelligence, they were an even match, but my father had the educational credentials that Sadie lacked, and which were so desirable in an upwardly mobile immigrant community. For her part, Sadie had the street smarts and the *chutzpah* that he would never acquire.

They began to see each other regularly, delighting in each other's company and my father anglicized Sadie's name by calling her Sally. She was so charmed by this that from then on she always introduced herself as Sally. But there was a major obstacle to this developing liaison: my father happened not to be Jewish, and within the generally bigoted British population, he had managed to encounter in the Cohen family a smaller group with its own equally strong sense of bigotry. Sally knew instantly that my father's religion was going to be a serious problem, but one of her favorite cliches was 'Where there's a will, there's a way!' Sally always had a will.

At first they met in secret, and only Sally's sister, Esther, knew about the budding romance. Esther could be trusted because she had her own shame to bear within the community: she was divorced. But as it became clear to my father and Sally that they were locked into a serious affair, she gradually leaked the story to her brothers and sisters until only my grandmother knew nothing of it.

*

J.K.C. Megahy in the 1920's

Sadie Cohen in the 1920's

In fact, my father's character and charm were such that he quickly overcame the Cohen family's natural suspicions of any *goy*; before long he became their treasured friend and confidant.

Years later, when one of my Aunt Esther's daughters, my cousin Alma, was in her late seventies and living in Israel, I wrote to her asking if it had ever occurred to her that my father might be of African descent. She replied:

Dear Francis

I am going to tell you a story. There was a very sick little girl, who had diphtheria, a killer in those days, but fortunately her aunt's fiancé was a doctor [my father]. *Three or four times a day he came to the house to swab and paint her throat. She therefore didn't have to go to Hospital. She called him 'Docky'.*

After his marriage to her aunt, he became Uncle Ken. He tried to persuade her mum to let him help her with the 'little girl's' education, he fancied she should be a doctor, but her mother was too proud to accept what could be looked on as a luxury. The war came and on his way to India, in Africa Uncle Ken bought two watches, one for his wife and one for the 'little girl'. I think he loved her as much as she loved him.

After the war she married and who did she choose to stand with her under the Chuppah – Uncle Ken. Soon after our marriage he was distressed by our carving knife and went and bought a 'good one' and sent it to us. For fifty-three years every time we used that carving knife we talked of Uncle Ken.

He was much loved and highly respected. I vaguely remember someone mentioning his skin, I think it was Ethel [her cousin], *Constance* [her sister] *said it was*

Gabie [another cousin], but did it really matter, Francis, if he was black, white, blue, yellow or even spotted?

For a person of her generation and background, this was a very broadminded view, but the Cohen family was much more outward-looking and unconventional than many others in Hightown.

My Uncle Barney for example, was a bookie, and in my recollection, a man permanently in debt. 'If you owe people money, son,' he would counsel me with a broad grin, 'don't worry about it! They're the ones who should be worrying about it!' Uncle Barney loved saying that.

Uncle Israel was a green-grocer and fishmonger, selling his fish and vegetables from a highly disorganized store, at the back of which he kept his horse and cart, which comprised the mobile store that he toured the neighborhood with. That long-suffering animal wasn't the only horse in his life: he spent a good deal of his time and money betting on other horses, with a particular fondness for the local racing specialty, trotting races.

Uncle Jack, a bad-tempered charmer with an eye for the ladies, and Uncle Solly, a gifted entrepreneur, were in the clothing business, and for a while they had operated in Canada. Solly always saw to it that my grandmother never had to think about money.

Most important of all for the cause of Sally and Ken, her brother Solly had already 'married out'. His wife, Ray, was an elegant and stunningly beautiful blue-eyed blonde *shicksa*, with a rich, rural Lancashire accent, who had willingly converted to Judaism. The Cohen family, like virtually all Jews in Britain at that time, was Orthodox, and conversion, being *magired* as it was known in Hightown, was no easy matter. You can get some idea of the difficulties from these suggestions from a contemporary guide to conversion, which recommends the following steps to any would-be convert:

Find a Rabbi. Some traditional Rabbis may actively discourage potential converts by turning them away three times. This is a test of how sincere the would-be convert is in wishing to become Jewish.

After finding a Rabbi, there is a period of study to learn such matters as Jewish beliefs, rituals, and prayers. This study might involve working directly with a rabbi or study in a conversion or introduction-to-Judaism class.

Orthodox Rabbis require a male candidate for conversion to have a circumcision.

Orthodox Rabbis require all candidates for conversion to go to a ritual bath called a mikveh.

The candidate for conversion appears before a Beth Din, or religious court, consisting of three learned people to see that all the steps of the conversion process have been done properly.

A Hebrew name is chosen. Sometimes there is a public ceremony celebrating the conversion.

Circumcision alone, no minor matter for any male past infancy, was an excellent test of a male candidate's seriousness. But it was obvious to Sally that if Ray had been able to convert, and her mother and the rest of the family had been able to accept Ray, well, my father could also be embraced by them.

Starting at Howard, and continuing through his experiences in St Lucia, and his return to the US and

NYU, he had developed a life as a loner, a man without friends. This certainly had its roots in his feelings of alienation after the shock of his arrival at Ellis Island and his treatment as a social inferior.

He had learned to live his life constantly on guard and his decision to 'pass' had only intensified his vigilance for any small miss-step that might lead whites to challenge him.

In close friendships it might have been more difficult to keep a consistent account of his life; at any moment a careless statement could lead to discovery. Friendship carried its temptations, but also its risks; who knew when a chance revelation of his secret might reveal a closet bigot?

But in Hightown, he was surprised to find that far from being scrutinized, he was celebrated, a man with more education and sophistication than almost anyone else in the community.

The Cohen brothers instinctively liked my father; they all had an adventurous streak as well as a natural immigrant instinct for survival, and they took to him, admiring his education and intellectual way of thinking, which they lacked, and above all his low-key manner and kindness.

From the Cohens, my father got the unconditional respect he had struggled for all his life; I never saw him more at ease than when he was in the company of the Cohen family.

Perhaps in a bizarre way, style excluded, the warmth of this large Jewish family reminded him of the warmth and comfort of his family and friends in Barbados in that uncorroded early part of his life, when the hurts and evasions of the future were unimaginable.

Although he shared no heritage or life experience with any of the Cohens, there was of course something crucial they did have in common: he too was an immigrant. As a group, the family were outsiders in Britain, and my father was an outsider as an individual — although to a far greater degree than any of the Cohens could have guessed.

The fact that he was a doctor played no small part in their acceptance of him. All through the Depression, the Cohen boys managed to make a living somehow, and they probably thought that my father's choice of a medical career was a shrewd one because it insulated him from the vagaries of the economy. Having a doctor as a brother-in-law would also flatter their own notions of upward mobility, and besides, he was going to take their spinster sister off their hands.

But he retained enough of his outsider image, his world-traveled urbanity and his intellectual curiosity, to maintain an undoubted glamor for Sally, which was to last the whole of their married life.

As he courted her, he would take her to the French restaurant of the Midland Hotel, then the best restaurant in the north of England, which she found exciting, but where she had difficulty choosing a dish that did not contravene the strict Jewish dietary laws. After dinner, they would dance. Sally was an enthusiastic dancer all her life. My father was a reluctant partner, but when she insisted, he always complied, and moved with a certain shy elegance. In the US, he had learned that it did not pay to draw attention to himself, to be exposed to any kind of scrutiny, so that in dancing as in everything else in his life, he remained resolutely low-key.

*

14 Marriage

My cousin Constance is in her eighties and still lives in Manchester, and she recalls my father virtually from the day he met my mother. I recently asked her if she had any idea where he came from, and she said, 'It was Canada, wasn't it?' Of course, I now know that he didn't come from Canada, but that was of course the story he told the whole Cohen family.

When he talked to Sally about his past life, it was easy for him to be very convincing because he could describe in great detail so many experiences that were true. He freely admitted that he had been to high school in Barbados, claiming that his father's work as a civil engineer had led the family to move there from its home in Canada for a few years; and of course, his time in Nova Scotia and in Winnipeg, meant that he could talk about Canada in detail. He said that he had studied medicine in New York, his parents had lived on the Upper West Side, and after that he returned to Canada to get his Canadian medical degree; and then he had decided to live in Britain, hence his degree from Edinburgh. All true.

It was what he did not talk about that would have exposed him. But in any case, Sally had fallen in love with a man who could transform her life, and it was hardly in her interest to challenge him.

He was on pretty safe ground with the invention of his Canadian birth. At a glance, with his olive skin, nobody would have thought he was British, but neither was there anything in his crisp profile to suggest that he was of African descent. Crucially, they had no one to compare him with. Even today there are only about half a million dark-skinned people in Britain, and almost all of them have arrived since the 1950's. In the 1920's, when my father met my mother, there were only a few thousand black people in Britain, and it's likely that nobody my father came into contact with in Manchester had ever seen a black person. I myself never saw one single person of African descent until I was twelve years old.

There's no way of knowing exactly what my father told Sally about his past; my only certainty is that he didn't tell her the truth. Even for a rebellious character like her, marrying a man of black African descent would have been an unacceptable outrage in 1930's Hightown. As for her family, it was possible that they could have accepted a religious convert, but Sadie marrying a *schwartzer* – a descendant of slaves! I don't think so.

It was my father's vast charm, his abilities and his ardor that won over my grandmother — as long as he was prepared to go through the laborious process of converting to Judaism. He certainly was, and thus he 'became' Jewish. A famous paragraph of the Talmud reads:

Dearer to God than all of the Israelites who stood at Mount Sinai is the convert. Had the Israelites not witnessed the lightning, thunder, and quaking mountain, and had they not heard the sounds of the shofar, they would not have accepted the Torah. But the convert, who did not see or hear any of these things, surrendered to God and accepted the yoke of heaven. Can anyone be dearer to God than such a person? [28]

This didn't fit my father very well. The cloak of

Judaism he slipped so easily around his shoulders was transparent. I can't recall his Hebrew name; I'm not even sure that he could recall it himself! Clearly he had not been passionate about his Christianity, and even as a child it was obvious to me that he was less than lukewarm about his Judaism. My own apathy in regard to religion definitely has its origins right here. My father had not suddenly seen some kind of Light; he simply wanted to marry his vivacious and sexy girlfriend, and if paying lip service to another form of worship was what it took, well, that was all right with him.

In 1941, when he was home on leave from his service in World War Two, we were staying in the old house in Thirlmere Street with my grandmother. That last week that my father spent in Manchester happened to be a week during which the Germans intensified their bombing campaign of Manchester's munitions factories and its Ship Canal, a vital waterway. During that week, there was a Luftwaffe bombing raid in the middle of the night and as we fearfully heard the distant explosions, my mother dragged me and my grandmother down from our bedrooms and into the coal cellar, theoretically a safer location. My father refused to join us.

Worried and infuriated, my mother called up to him, 'Ken! Are you mad? For God's sake come down here!'

I can still hear his cheerful, confident voice calling back, 'It's the same God up here as it is down there, Sally — I'm going to sleep in my bed!'

It took me years to understand that he meant that for him there was *no* God either upstairs or down. Whatever the religion, everything I remember about him tells me that he was not a believer of any kind. And that was that; he wasn't scared like the rest of us, he was always so low key, that this was the first time that I ever realized how determined a character my father was.

But apart from marrying Sadie, he did have another very good motive for his religious conversion: for a man who was eager to camouflage his real racial heritage, the adoption of Judaism provided a welcome extra layer of disguise. With this, he had managed to distance himself a few important steps even further away from his true antecedents. How could anybody have thought a Jewish man was a negro? No, he was now a Jewish Canadian doctor.

My father had discovered an ingenious way to enjoy the best of two worlds, both theoretically denied to him: he had become a member of a community that admired and nurtured him, and of a family that embraced him fully – and without allowing Judaism to be imposed on him in any way. I can't recollect him attending a single service in the *schul* that was not a special family occasion.

And outside the ghetto, in the gentile community, beyond the few self-conscious square miles of Hightown, his appearance gave nobody any reason to think that he was either Jewish or black. So as long as he stuck to his fake life story, and made no revealing slips, he could pass effortlessly wherever he chose to go.

*

15 My Parents' Wedding – And My Birth

My father and Sally were duly married in 1933, and by that time my father had developed his own medical practice in Salford. The wedding itself was unusual, to say the least. In the calendar of Jewish family life, a wedding is a hugely important event, an opportunity for the clans to gather and celebrate themselves.

In my childhood, weddings seemed to be endless; I sweated through so many evenings in thick suits, eating through interminable dinners where the 'non-dairy' dessert, respecting the rules of the Beth Din about not mixing meat and milk dishes, never failed to disappoint. The entire families of both the bride and groom would be present, playing out for real the drama and comedy of old enmities, familiar from so many plays and movies about Jewish life.

But Sally and my father had no such event. They were not even married in Manchester. They had a civil wedding in London, their honeymoon a scant few days in a hotel in Victoria. Try as I might, I have never found one family member who remembers their wedding, and no photographs survive. Until I began researching this book, I had never thought about my parents' wedding photographs; now, knowing the Cohens as I do, it's clearly very strange that there were no photographs. I think that my father persuaded Sally that it would be a romantic gesture to elope to London and on their return, present the family with a fait accompli...

This apparently worked out as he had planned. By this time, the Cohens loved him, but they also knew that he was unconventional, and he could get away with behavior they could not. My father moved into the house in Thirlmere Street, with my mother and grandmother, and I was born in March, 1935, in that house.

A father's first sight of his child is always an emotional event, but the actual moment of my birth was especially traumatic for my father. With his three medical degrees, he knew enough about genetics to know only too well that there was every chance that I could have been born with a dark skin. How on earth would he have explained a black baby to my mother and her Jewish family in 1930's Manchester!

In 2011, I made a trip to Manchester, to talk to the oldest people in my family, to see if they had any recollections about my father that would throw a fresh light on him. We sat around in my cousin Harry's living room, drinking sweet, milky hot tea, and I tried to prod the small group into remembering anything, however trivial.

My oldest cousin, Gertie, a stooped lady in her eighties, suddenly said, 'Well, I was in the house when you were born.' That caught my interest. I knew that I was born not in a hospital but in my grandmother's house in Hightown.

'I didn't know you were there,' I said.

'Oh, yes,' she said, 'I was there. Your father delivered you.'

I was astonished to hear this, because it was against all medical ethics, due to the opportunities it creates for someone unscrupulous to get rid of a child. It was equally surprising because my birth certificate was not signed by my father, but by his friend, the Cohen family doctor, Dr Hirson. I now heard that Hirson had not even been in the building at the crucial moment.

Indeed, when I returned to Los Angeles, I searched yet again through every last piece of paper related to my parents and found a small crumpled note, written in April 1935 to my father:

409 Cheetham Hill Road
Manchester, 8
Dear Dr & Mrs Megahy
I want to thank you most sincerely for the beautiful gift you kindly sent me. I really appreciate your kind thoughts, your beautiful present will always remind me of the little romance which happened during your acting as locum to me with the ultimate result that I was again of some service.

Again thanking you & hope that Mrs Megahy and Baby are now enjoying the best of health.

Yours very sincerely
Edward Hirson

*

It was clear why my father made sure that he delivered me himself. He had to protect himself and my mother against any chance that this new baby might not have a white skin. The impact of seeing her black baby could have been enough to kill my mother on the spot. I'm sure that if the 'worst' happened, my father wanted to be alone with her to explain how a nice Jewish lady had produced a *schwartzer* baby! I cannot imagine what he would have done or how he could have talked his way out of the situation, but fortune favored him, and no explanations – or actions – were necessary.

I asked Cousin Gertie how my father had reacted when I was born. 'Naturally, he was excited, wanted to take you for a ride in his car straightaway! Pleased as Punch he was,' she said. 'He would be, wouldn't he!'

Oh, yes, he would be: because beneath what onlookers saw as the usual, predictable excitement of a new father, he concealed an incredible sense of relief: he had produced a child who looked one hundred per cent white. His life was going well; he had his white wife, and now his white son. Before I was twenty-four hours old, he took me out for a drive in his car, infecting me for ever with his own love of motor vehicles.

Living with my grandmother might have been a convenient arrangement, but it was certainly was not the life style he had in mind. As in the rest of Manchester, and indeed the whole of the industrial north of England, every building, tree and blade of grass was soot-blackened from the factory smoke-stacks and the coal fires that heated every home. There was little entertainment in Manchester, few good restaurants, only one quality theatre. Strangely, the liveliest part of the town was the ghetto, but my father had lived in New York and London, and had no intention of spending the rest of his life in Hightown.

My mother was very close with her family and would have many conflicting feelings about moving away from them. Nevertheless, when I was eighteen months old, we moved eighty miles away, to Leicester, another industrial city, which was possibly even gloomier than Manchester.

My parents rented a comfortable house in a Leicester suburb. As I recall it, through my infant's eyes, compared with my grandmother's house, it was huge.

I don't know why my father and mother decided to move to Leicester. I'm sure that all along my father wanted to live in a city where nobody knew him, and where he was free from even the remote possibility of anyone in or around the Cohen family prying into his past. Perhaps too he felt that he had mollify both his wife and her family by moving away in stages. There was, after all, no practical reason, like a job, which made leaving Manchester an imperative: it was a move of choice.

But after only a year in Leicester, we moved again, this time to the real thing: London. I was too young to recall any family discussions about where we were going to live, and I can only speculate about their reasons for moving to London. My mother certainly could have had no special attachment for Leicester, but London, now that spelled excitement and a really new life.

Or perhaps they each had different reasons. For my mother, there was no Jewish community in Leicester, and she had lived all her life in the narrow confines of an exclusively Jewish world. Like many immigrants, she sought the comfort of people like herself; in London there were famous Jewish sections of the city. But my father was an outsider wherever he went, and he loved the life of a major city. On her brief honeymoon, my mother had come to share his love of the glamour of London and its theaters and restaurants.

But the city's attractions were probably superficial reasons for the family move; for my father, the crucial matter was that we were now a unit on our own, more self-contained, less likely to be questioned or examined.

We were some two hundred miles from Manchester, living in a world apart from Hightown, and despite my father's embrace of Hightown, his conversion to Judaism, and his well-reciprocated affection for his wife's family, he made sure that we never again lived in the same city as they did.

*

16   Dr Kenneth Megahy – London

We moved to a part of London that was decidedly unglamorous, East Ham, a sprawling working class development, built along the river Thames for factory and dock workers in a boom at the end of the nineteenth century, when the East End of London was a major industrial center, and the biggest commercial port in Europe. In East Ham, the houses were as black and the air as unpalatable as in Hightown.

My father bought a medical practice there. This was some ten years before the establishment of Britain's National Health Service. Before that, medical practices were bought and sold much as a shoe store or hardware store might be, but in this case the goodwill was the list of patients. This was always a risky purchase: the selling doctor could make no guarantees that the patients would like the incoming doctor; and they were quite free to move to a new doctor, taking the so-called goodwill with them as they walked out the door.

But if there was one area of his life in which my father had total confidence, it was in his medical skills. He had more than one medical degree, had always been a brilliant student, fascinated by the techniques and technology of medicine, and he brought to his work the innate skills of a perceptive intelligence and an intuitive, sympathetic manner.

When he bought the practice in East Ham, he also took over the previous doctor's old office, a small two-story store front; when we first arrived in London, we lived above the store. The ground floor was a converted shop: the original shop area had been made into a waiting room, behind that, the shop's store room became my father's office for seeing patients and there was a small room he called the Dispensary, where in those pre-National Health Service days, he kept the prescription drugs he sold to the patients.

On the floor above was our living accommodation: a sitting room, my parents' bedroom, a single bathroom and my bedroom. Late one afternoon, when I was three years old, I was riding my tricycle along the upper floor and as I came to the top of the staircase, I saw my father at the bottom. 'Daddy!' I shouted and headed down to meet him, immediately losing my balance, sailing down the stairs end over end, almost knocking him down and smashing my chin against the handlebars. My mother, running to find out the reason for my yelling and crying, saw the crash and screamed at the sight of my face dripping with blood.

Always calm, my father said, 'Take it easy, Sally. It's not that bad.'

'Not that bad! Look at all that blood, oh my God!'

'Just help me to carry him into the kitchen,' he said.

'Aren't you taking him to the hospital?'

'I *am* the hospital!' he said.

They laid me out on the kitchen table, he gave my mother a compress to press on my bleeding chin, and then went back to his office. His early medical career had accustomed him to dealing with serious injuries in areas of the world where there were no hospitals.

Returning with his 'sewing kit', he told my mother,'I don't think you want to watch this,' well knowing how squeamish she was. 'You should go back upstairs, Sally, he'll be all right.' She took his advice.

He quickly gave me an injection to numb the area around the cut on my chin and calmly started to sew it up. Soothed by his calm and confident tone, I stopped crying and he sewed up the gash so skillfully that today I have only the faintest scar to remind me of that dizzying fall. A strange bonding experience. Yes, even in my earliest memories, there was much about him to compel my love and admiration.

We only lived in East Ham for a year. It was not an attractive part of London, the small row houses created a drab and monotonous landscape, and the air itself, polluted by the huge Tate and Lyle sugar processing plant, by smoke from the steamships in the docks, and noxious fumes from the Gas, Light and Coke Company's refinery, had an unhealthy tang. As soon as they could afford it, my parents rented a pleasant house with a garden, in Chingford, at the very edge of the city, near Epping Forest. I have only a few, hazy images of that house: tall trees at the end of a lawn and a pointed roof over the front door, which I now suppose was a Victorian Gothic porch.

Every day we drove to the office, where my mother fielded phone calls, kept the books, and sometimes dispensed the drugs that my father sold to his patients.

Dr Megahy's office was open in the morning and in the late afternoon, and in between he made his house calls and visited those patients who were in hospital. He came home for lunch, my mother cooked, and we all ate together. When he closed his office at the end of the day, we all drove back to Chingford, always with my mother telling him to slow down.

Our life settled into a comfortable pattern. My father made frequent trips into the city, shopping with my mother, or on his own to surprise her with gifts or something for the house. They went out to restaurants in Soho for dinner, dragging me along with them, and to the theatre; my mother adored musicals and they saw every one as soon as it opened. Among her favorites were Noel Coward's *The Dancing Years* and Cole Porter's *Anything Goes.*

My father loved hardware stores, and when he occasionally took me with him, we would make straight for a big department store, Gamages in Holborn, where the kitchen and hardware departments took up almost the whole if its basement. He loved gadgets of any kind, and was a sucker for any new kind of can opener, or blender, or mincer. I was fascinated by these devices, but my mother disliked all things mechanical, from cars on down, and sooner or later would disable, destroy or deliberately lose his latest gadget.

My father would find himself trying to use the old, primitive can opener that my mother was perfectly happy with, and ask, 'Why are we using this damn thing, Sally? What happened to the new one I bought in Gamages?'

'It broke!' she'd say, muttering, 'It was no better anyway…'

My father would pretend that he didn't hear her, and she would pretend that she didn't see him shaking his head, and they'd both let it go. This didn't mean he wouldn't turn up a week later carrying a vast and complex bread slicer!

One of our biggest excitements came in the spring of 1939 when we got a second car. When we first arrived in London, my father bought a two year old

1935 Morris, a small economy car *[29]*. But the Morris was just a stopgap, and he became very excited when two years later, he had enough money for a new car. It was a Rover 14 Sports Saloon, a small quality car of the day with a long hood, shimmering dark blue paint, a tan interior, and that intoxicating 'new car smell' that emanated from all leather-trimmed cars of the period. Even today, if I get a whiff of that smell, it instantly brings back a vivid image of that blue Rover 14 *[30]*.

My mother liked the car, but was a little uneasy about the expense of having two cars, especially as she had not the slightest intention of driving either of them, but my father insisted that living so far from his office, he had to be certain that if one car broke down, the other would be available. But really, it was just that he loved cars, and if he could have found a pretext and the money, we might have ended up with three or four!

On Sundays we often drove from Chingford back into the city, to the heart of the old Jewish East End, to Petticoat Lane, a long narrow street market, lined with stalls and thronged with so many customers that it was hard to walk even in the middle of the street.

My father would carry me on his shoulders through the market, pushing our way through the crowd, my mother protesting, 'He's too heavy, Ken, you'll drop him!' He just laughed and so did I, my head above the crowd, a very cosmopolitan crowd, which was probably why he felt at home there.

We went into what I remember as an enormous delicatessen, sacks of flour and lentils and rice on the floor, giant hunks of cheese on the marble counter next to jars of gefilte fish and pickles, and bowls swimming with pickled cucumbers.

One morning, as my mother began to go through her shopping list, my father asked the shopkeeper to cut off a fresh chunk of Gouda cheese, carved out from a big red-waxed wheel, just off the boat from Amsterdam – and gave it to me. 'You'll like this,' he said.

I took it reluctantly, looking at suspiciously. It was squashy and I didn't like the feel of it. He laughed at the look on my face, and said, 'Go on, sonny, try it!' Gingerly, I bit off a small piece, and it was the beginning of my lifelong love for Gouda, the soft, creamy Dutch cheese. Even now, just one bite takes me back to that Petticoat Lane shop.

My father laughed at the expressions on my face, turning from suspicion to enjoyment. As I ate the cheese, I laughed too, not sure what I was laughing at, but enjoying laughing with my father.

'What are you two laughing at!' my mother said sharply, almost caricaturing herself. 'Ken, stop it! People will think you're mad, the pair of you!'

We just laughed all the more and she started laughing too, the sharp pretense dissolved.

'Can somebody tell me what we're laughing at?' she asked, and of course, that set us all off again.

We may have been laughing, but the year was 1939, and our world, like that of all Europeans, was about to be turned upside down. Of course I knew nothing of Neville Chamberlain's failed encounter with Adolf Hitler in Munch, or even that later in the summer we would be at war. I knew there was something called a war, but I had no idea what the word meant.

That changed in 1940, when the war came to have a

mysterious reality for me. I was in the kitchen in East Ham, with my mother, watching her boiling water for hot tea, and listening to the radio. Through the kitchen window, I could see some huge, tethered objects, swaying gently a few hundred feet above the ground. I loved the look of them, like vast inflated toy elephants, but they were in fact barrage balloons, enormous inflatables tethered to the ground at low level in the hope of deterring the German bombers from low-level bombing runs.

Then something on the radio abruptly caught my mother's attention, and she stopped what she was doing. Then she said, 'Oh, my God!' and the tea-pot slipped from her fingers, fell, and almost in slow motion, shattered on the tile floor, the fragments of pottery seeming to bounce and the hot water running everywhere. She leaned back on the kitchen counter, stunned and scared. My father walked quickly into the kitchen, asking, 'What is it, what happened?'

I remember my mother's exact reply, although I had no idea what one of the words meant, or what this piece of news meant. She said, 'France has capitulated!'

'Oh, that's not good news,' said my father, stooping to clear up the floor. 'But we'll be all right.'

I watched them hug, and I knew this 'capitulated' was something bad. It was June 10th. By the 12th the Germans were in Paris, and a week later they had reached the French coast. Twenty-one miles of ocean was all that separated them from us.

Six months earlier, in the hope of making night-time navigation difficult for German bombers, the British Government had imposed a Blackout on the entire country. There were to be no car headlights, no lights in store windows, no lighted office windows, and no light coming from homes. Putting up the blackout sheets was a tedious chore, but people were motivated by fear. The regulations were enforced by the ever-present patrols of Air Raid Prevention Wardens, there were heavy fines for anyone giving the enemy the slightest clue about where they were, and the Blackout was very quickly one hundred per cent accomplished.

At night, I recall how spooky the city was, little traffic, a ghostly feeling in the deserted, pitch-black streets, just a few pedestrians fumbling their way in the dark, an occasional slow-moving car with dimmed and hooded headlights.

Even for a five year old, hearing only snatches of the grown-ups' quiet conversations on the street or in shops, or in news reports on the radio, the atmosphere of fear that gripped London in that summer of 1940 became palpable. I didn't know what exactly was going on, but I knew that people were scared.

Hitler had assembled more than two thousand barges at his new bases on the French coast to ferry the German troops across the Channel for a large-scale invasion of Britain. On August 12th, the German bombing campaign started, designed to soften up the British defenses before the invasion itself.

Resisting the German bombers became a life and death matter for everyone in Britain, and the fierce aerial battle that ensued became known as the Battle of Britain.

On weekends, in the garden in Chingford, I watched until my neck ached as the German bombers tried to reach the London docks, and the RAF fighters tried to stop them. The bombers had fighter escorts, Messerschmidt ME 109's, and furious aerial battles began between them and the British Hurricanes and Spitfires. The fighter planes wheeled and rolled and dived, exchanging bursts of machine-gun fire, and every now and them one of them would fall from the sky, trailing flames and a thickening plume of smoke. Interspersed with the heavy rattle of the fighters' .50 calibre machine guns was the occasional dull thud of a bomb hitting the ground.

The RAF was losing pilots and planes faster than they could be trained and manufactured, but the supply of German bombers seemed limitless. The news on the radio took on an even grimmer tone. Falling asleep, I heard my parents arguing late one night.

'They need doctors, Sally,' my father said.

'All right, I know that,' said my mother, 'but why do you have to volunteer? Can't you wait till they call you up?'

'No, I can't. They need doctors *right now*!'

'Volunteer' was a new and puzzling word, but I soon found out what it meant when I was told a couple of days later that my father was joining the army. I thought it sounded exciting, having no idea how our lives were going to change.

I marvel at my father's decision. He was 55, and he must have known the extent of the jeopardy to which he was exposing himself. Was he motivated by patriotism, by repugnance for the Nazi ideology, indeed, how much did he know of the Nazi party's racist views? Did he feel personally threatened by the prospect of Britain being occupied by a regime determined to stamp out those whose racial heritage was contaminated? I'll never know, it was yet another subject we never talked about. I only know that he saw it as his plain and simple obligation to do whatever he could to defend his adopted country.

This was not a distant war like Korea, not a reckless adventure like invading Iraq, this was a terrifying, living, breathing threat right on our doorstep, and the British were prepared to fight to the death to avoid German occupation. It was dramatized by Winston Churchill's powerful and inspiring speech in the House of Commons on June 4th:

'...we shall fight on the seas and oceans, we shall fight with growing confidence and growing strength in the air, we shall defend our island, whatever the cost may be. We shall fight on the beaches, we shall fight on the landing grounds, we shall fight in the fields and in the streets, we shall fight in the hills; we shall never surrender!'

I was five years old. Did I know what this speech meant? Huddled around the radio with my mother and father, I certainly knew the impact the speech had, that we were in mortal danger.

In the second week in July, the week after the Battle of Britain started in earnest, my father became Captain Megahy, Royal Army Medical Corps. His first posting was in Kent, a county south of London, in the direct line of flight for the Luftwaffe bombers crossing the Channel from their new French bases, and this was where the fiercest aerial battles took place. My father was assigned an ambulance, a driver and a nurse, and their task was simple: they waited for information about planes that crashed or were shot down, or about airman who had bailed out and parachuted to the ground, and then they drove as near to the scene as they could get, where Captain Megahy could work on the downed pilots, if they had survived.

He only gave my mother the briefest description of how he spent his days, and never talked of them even years after the war. Later, when I read about the Battle of Britain, I learned that many of the German and British pilots, young men barely out of their teens, suffered extensive burns and other horrible injuries.

Throughout that summer, we hardly saw my father. The bombing and the fighting continued seven days a week, there was no leave for Army doctors, and we were discouraged from making a visit to Kent.

The Battle was tough – the life expectancy of an RAF Spitfire or Hurricane pilot averaged 87 flying hours [31], but by the late summer, the small RAF fighter planes were gaining the upper hand, prompting another celebrated Churchill speech, an exhilarating commendation of those brave young flyers for their sacrifice. The speech echoed Shakespeare's Henry V as he exhorted his men to fight for their country before the battle of Agincourt. As we would on so many other occasions, my mother and I were transfixed by the great man's oratory:

'The gratitude of every home in our Island, in our Empire, and indeed throughout the world, except in the abodes of the guilty, goes out to the British airmen who, undaunted by odds, unwearied in their constant challenge and mortal danger, are turning the tide of the World War by their prowess and by their devotion. Never in the field of human conflict was so much owed by so many to so few. All our hearts go out to the

fighter pilots, whose brilliant actions we see with our own eyes day after day...' [32]

I knew from Churchill's stirring tone of voice, and the effect that his speech had on my mother, that this was powerful stuff. I knew that my father was somehow part of this struggle, but I didn't understand exactly how.

Only two years later, these efforts were celebrated in a movie of the period, *The First of the Few*, describing how the Spitfire was developed by its designer, RJ Mitchell, and covering its Battle of Britain exploits. The movie became a favorite of mine, and since that date, I've always loved the Spitfire, the most graceful, elegant and aerobatic of the Word War Two fighter planes.

By October 1940, the RAF had won the Battle of Britain. It wasn't the end of German bombing, but the brave young fliers had prevented the terrifying threat of an immediate invasion, and Hitler ignored the advice of his generals, and decided to turn his attention to his doomed attempt to conquer Russia.

My father was no longer needed in Kent; he was soon promoted to Major and with the privileges of that rank he acquired a batman and a driver. As troops were assembled in different locations all over Great Britain, my father had a series of postings to different cities, running Army Hospitals. Whenever possible, we followed him.

One of his longer postings was in Wales and I was sent to school there. Every day my mother put me on a small train for the short ride from Conway to Colwyn Bay, where someone from the school met me and several other children.

But one day when I got off the train there were no other children, and nobody from the school to meet me. I started walking, in what I thought was the direction of the school, but I couldn't find it. Eventually, hot, tired and worried, I found my way back to the railway station.

I saw a policeman standing outside the station, casually watching people boarding the trains. I didn't want to embarrass myself by admitting that I was in trouble, but I had to do something, so I walked up to him, and asked, 'What would you do, if you were lost?'

'I'd ask a policeman, boyo!' he said and laughed cheerfully. 'Now, what's your name, and where are you from, sonny?'

An hour later my father's Army driver rolled up, and looked at me with some relief. 'We were all very worried about you!' he said. 'Well, all of us except the Major, he was sure you'd be all right.'

I asked him if I could sit in the front of the car. 'No, you can't,' he said. 'You sit in the back and keep your head down, official vehicles aren't supposed to be used for finding lost little boys!'

Later, in 1941, my father was sent to run a hospital in Yorkshire, in a small wool town, Elland, nestled in the Yorkshire Moors. My mother rented a couple of rooms in a very pleasant Victorian house on the edge of the town, and I went to yet another school, walking every day through the wool mills, with their huge, stacked bales of raw wool waiting to be processed. A smell I'll never forget.

My father came home for dinner most evenings, but he had to sleep at the hospital. Elland is in a valley, and one of the most exciting features of it for me was the trolley buses, my first experience of these quiet, electric vehicles, which took me and my mother to the neighboring larger city of Halifax I had made a wooden model of a Halifax bomber, not from a kit, but from scraps of wood I found and my mother entered it in a competition. My mother and father were thrilled when it won the best prize in my age group. The next week my name was in the local paper, and my mother heard from my father's driver that the soldiers at the hospital had already grown tired of him taking the cutting from his pocket and showing it to them!

Years later, after my father's death, I found that he had kept the model Halifax, in one his many boxes of old papers and souvenirs. I was surprised how shoddy an effort it was, but I suppose it wasn't bad for a six year old, and it clearly meant a great deal to him.

In May, our Yorkshire sojourn came to an end with the announcement that my father was being posted to the Middle East. He was given a week's 'embarkation leave' and we spent it in my grandmother's house in Manchester.

While he was there, he went to visit my cousin Audrey, a young woman in her twenties, who had come down with some unidentified illness and was in a local hospital, The Royal Infirmary, almost two hundred years old. The family was worried about Audrey, she didn't seem to be getting better, and my father decided that he'd better go and check what was happening. Since he was only home for a week, and wanted to spend as much time as he could with me, he took me with him.

It was the first time I had ever been in a hospital,

and I didn't like it. I didn't like the institutional smell, and I didn't like the feeling that this was a place where bad things happened. Audrey lay inert in bed, with a high fever and not breathing well. But she immediately brightened at the sound of my father's voice. 'Uncle Ken! I'm really poorly, and they don't know what's wrong with me, I'm so pleased to see you.'

He held her hand as he checked her temperature. 'I have to go and talk to Audrey's doctor,' he said to me. 'You can hold her hand, I'll only be a few minutes.'

I approached the bed reluctantly.

'Go ahead, man!' he said, smiling. 'She won't bite you!'

A few minutes later he returned with a doctor. 'I have to make an apology to you, Miss Cohen,' he said. 'We may not have been giving you exactly the right medicine.'

Her illness had been completely misdiagnosed, and in those carefree days before medical malpractice lawsuits, that was all the apology she was going to get. Behind him, my father, whose great instinct for diagnosis had led him to the hospital's error, was nodding.

When we got back to Thirlmere Street, my mother asked what had happened, but he wouldn't give her any details. 'Professional courtesy,' he said. 'They were wrong, but they did their best, Sally. She'll be fine.'

Audrey made a rapid recovery and came out of the hospital a few days after my father's leave was over.

*

17 My Father Leaves For The Middle East

Once my father was due to leave the country, there was nothing to keep us in East Ham or Chingford. The Chingford lease was running out, the office in East Ham was locked and everything put in storage, including my father's prized possession, his Rover.

We saw my father off at Waterloo Station, as he caught a train with hundreds of other men in uniform, for Southampton. My mother cried, but I was excited. I knew he was going away, and that we couldn't go with him, but that was all. In the past two years, my father had often been away from home for short periods, and this simply felt like more of the same. I had no idea that I wouldn't see him for three years.

We moved back to Manchester, back to Hightown again, to the familiarity of Thirlmere Street, to live in my grandmother's house.

I'm told that my grandmother was a warm and loving person, but I only remember her as a rather forbidding blind *babushka*, who always wore black clothing. In the movie *Rebecca*, one of the devices Hitchcock used to give the housekeeper, Mrs Danvers, a sinister presence, was that you never saw her enter or leave a room. Joan Fontaine would turn around, and find Mrs Danvers standing there – or she turned around, and she had vanished. I have no recollection of seeing my grandmother walk. I'm sure that, like all the Cohens, she was indeed warm and caring, but that isn't my memory of her. And I kept out of her way whenever I could.

*

My father spent most of his overseas service in India, learning to love Indian food, a taste I didn't share until my twenties. As the Commanding Officer of a Motor Ambulance Convoy, he was promoted to Colonel. I have wonderful photographs of him in India, standing next to his huge Humber Staff car under a jacaranda tree; and a bizarre studio shot where he is seated in his best tropical weight dress uniform, and next to him stands a young Indian man, quite elegant in his traditional clothes, wearing a fez, my father's tailor.

My father never saw action. I think the Army had decided that his skills and experience were of greatest use in running hospitals, mobile or otherwise, and they seemed to have no desire to send this man now approaching sixty into a combat zone.

Our only contact with him was through letters, and they were few and far between in each direction. We had to write our letters to him on a special Army form, and they were then photocopied and reduced in size, so that they took up less room to ship out to the solders.

After the war, I discovered that he had treasured my letters and kept them, tiny little notes measuring four inches by three, some of them illustrated with drawings of pirate ships or whatever took my fancy at the time.

My favorite one of these letters was a complaint about my mother, beseeching my father, as the presumed higher authority, to stop my mother eating most of the small pieces of cheese we got with our food coupons.

'I like shavings of cheese, and she likes chunks, so

she eats more cheese than I do!' my seven year old self complained. I can't remember if or how he settled this dispute.

I was seven years old but already the longest I had lived in one place was a year and a half.

My mother and I followed the war in great detail. I had already developed a love of movies so we went to the cinema at least once a week. I liked Westerns and adventures; Errol Flynn in *They Died with Their Boots On* was a favorite. My mother's taste ran to romantic movies, so we always saw Nelson Eddy and Jeanette McDonald musicals as well as weepy movies like *Mrs Miniver*.

But the War could not be escaped, even in the movie theaters. Before the features, there were always newsreels, and those newsreels always had a lot of war footage in them. I still have vivid images in my head of 'house-to-house' fighting, the soldiers struggling for towns and villages, building by building, doorway by doorway, alley by alley. My mother didn't like those newsreels; they were too graphic and they dramatized her fear for my father.

We thought that he was a long way from the action, but scarily, we couldn't be sure. The war's outcome remained uncertain, and it was never far from anybody's thoughts or conversation. Only one question was on my mother's mind: when was my father coming home?

*

My father in Madras with his Indian Tailor

My father in Bangalore with his Army Staff Car

My grandmother died in 1943, and her funeral was a big family event, with lots of wailing and crying. Then for the next week of ritual mourning, *Shivah*, we had to stay in the house and receive all comers. *Shivah* is actually a fine way for the family and their friends to share and accept the initial pain of bereavement, but as a restless child it drove me crazy. I was already developing my antipathy to religion, it always seemed to be so restrictive, always about what you couldn't do.

After my grandmother's death, my mother and I stayed on in the Thirlmere Street house and resumed the old routine. My mother made her own cream cheese, and I was sent each morning to Black's deli, around the corner, to bring back fresh and still-warm bagels for breakfast.

My father had been away for three years and had almost ceased to be a presence in my life. My mother still spoke about him all the time, as did all the Cohens, but now it was my mother who made all the rules and all the decisions about my life. When I disagreed with some ruling of my mother's – 'Time for bed – *now!*' – there was nobody to appeal to, nobody to intervene, no higher court. And because my mother had to handle everything on her own, she became more strict, more restrictive. I remembered my father's benevolence, I wondered if he would ever return.

Then in June, 1944, we got the news – and saw the newsreels – of the D Day landings on the beaches of Normandy. It looked as if the end of the war was in sight, but then the Germans counter-attacked and that led to the Allies' slog through the Belgian Ardennes, the Battle of the Bulge, the most brutal battle

Americans fought in the war, with 89,000 casualties.

Astonishingly, this was the moment when racism entered the equation. The punishing US losses meant that General Eisenhower was short of replacement troops. Up to this moment, most blacks in the US army were only allowed to be cleaners, truck drivers or dockers, but now in desperation, Eisenhower armed the black soldiers, and for the first time, they fought alongside white soldiers. The unintended consequence was a first step toward the racial integration of the US Military. *[33]*

Within a few months, the Allies' overwhelming air superiority overcame the Germans, and we listened to the last of Churchill's war-time speeches:

Hostilities will end officially at one minute after midnight to-night (Tuesday, May 7, 1945), but in the interests of saving lives the 'Cease fire' began yesterday to be sounded all along the front, and our dear Channel Islands are also to be freed to-day.

The German war is therefore at an end. After years of intense preparation, Germany hurled herself on Poland at the beginning of September, 1939; and, in pursuance of our guarantee to Poland and in agreement with the French Republic, Great Britain, the British Empire and Commonwealth of Nations, declared war upon this foul aggression. After gallant France had been struck down we, from this Island and from our united Empire, maintained the struggle single-handed for a whole year until we were joined by the military might of Soviet Russia, and later by the overwhelming power and resources of the United States of America.

Finally almost the whole world was combined

against the evil-doers, who are now prostrate before us. Our gratitude to our splendid Allies goes forth from all our hearts in this Island and throughout the British Empire.'

He concluded on a justifiably patriotic note:

'Advance, Britannia! Long live the cause of freedom! God save the King!'

The brief period of rejoicing kicked off with street parties all over the country. In truth, it was a special day for Jews, whose rejoicing at the suicide of the architect of the Final Solution was more than understandable.

I still remember the celebration on Thirlmere Street, smiles everywhere, kids running around and the adults letting them do it, the narrow cobbled street filled by tables covered with food – Jewish food. In a magnificent irony, we celebrated the Nazis defeat with *gefilte fish* and pickled herrings!

*

18 Manchester, My Father Returns From The War

The first time I ever remember traveling in a taxi was in September 1945, when my mother and I went to meet my father at Manchester's Victoria Station, when he returned to England after three years in India and Iraq.

The day before, when his military transport ship had docked in Southampton, he used his rank as Colonel to get to a phone quickly. My mother screamed with delight when she heard his voice, telling her that he'd be back in Manchester the next day.

When the taxi came to my grandmother's house to pick us up, neighbors peered out from behind their net curtains. In Thirlmere Street, taxis were only seen for weddings and funerals, and they knew we were not going to any of those. The taxi was a big Austin 16, dark green, with black wings, it was clean and quiet, and it was the nicest car I had ever been in.

My mother wore a red silk dress and a brown hat. I had on my best best blazer and long grey flannel trousers, very proud that I was wearing long trousers. It was more than three years since I'd seen my father, a long time in the life of a ten year old; I was beside myself with excitement and so was my mother.

We got to the station early, and stood around impatiently, watching the indicator board. Finally, with a big puff of steam, a cloud of smoke and loud squeals from its brakes, the train arrived. We stared eagerly at the crowd walking off the train, and suddenly, there was my father, looking tanned and healthy, striding vigorously toward us, with the broadest smile. He dropped his Army kitbag, and grabbed us both in a muscular hug, squashing me into his uniform. I immediately sensed an almost overpowering feeling of energy and affection from him.

He looked down at me. 'You *have* grown, son!' he said. I stared at him, not remembering him precisely, not knowing what to say, but very impressed. In the taxi we sat on either side of him for the short ride back to Thirlmere Street. I kept leaning forward, turning to look at him, examining him, and he felt my stare and smiled a dazzling smile down at me. I smiled back. We were all grinning like fools! The taxi stopped at number 16, we got out and as my father paid the driver, my mother caught me staring at him again.

She leaned down toward me and spoke quietly. 'What do you think?' she asked.

I replied with a line that made us all laugh for years afterwards, I said, 'He's not bad, is he...' I actually couldn't remember him that well, and meeting him was overwhelming.

When we got into the house, he started to talk enthusiastically about East Ham, how he wanted to get back to London, back to work and to our old life.

My mother cut him off, 'It's not going to be that easy, Ken.'

He frowned, 'Why not?' and she then gave him the bad news, which she had sensibly kept from him while he was away. German bombing had flattened the East Ham store front where we had first lived and where his doctor's office was. Nobody bothered to mention the fact that if we had remained there, we could have been bombed flat too!

We had also lost everything we had put into storage.

My father suddenly guessed why my mother had been keeping this information from him. 'Not the Rover!' he said, more disturbed about the loss of his beloved car than anything else. My mother smiled sadly, she knew how much that car meant to him, and said, 'Yes, the Rover too.'

'Oh, well,' he shrugged, 'At least we have the Morris.' I saw that his face was determined, and that he would not be deterred by a little Nazi bombing.

Fortunately, the small 1935 Morris 8, my father's emergency second car, now ten years old, had been stored in Hightown, in a stable owned by my Uncle Israel, the celebrated and well loved local character, who sold fish and vegetables from a horse-drawn cart as it clattered over the cobblestones of the ghetto.

My mother had prepared a special dinner for my father's return, full of black market ingredients. There was matzo ball soup, with dumplings, which he'd acquired a taste for, roast chicken with potatoes, and a favorite of my father's, rice and peas. It was not until fifty years later that I found out that rice and peas was a staple of Barbados cuisine. I ate and watched, and listened to their conversation, the man fascinated me.

After dinner, he handed out some gifts. For my mother there was intricately made gold jewelery from India; for me there was a wooden model of an Army ambulance made for me by one of the soldiers under his command. He also gave me a number of matchboxes, filled with sand and marked variously as *From the Arabian Desert, From Iraq, From Syria* and *From Libya.*

I hardly recall him talking about his war service, but when he did, it was obvious that he had enjoyed it.

He liked his Army work; he had a natural talent for organization and he was an expert medical improviser. He enjoyed the interaction with his subordinates, and above all, for the first time in his life, he was in a formal position of authority. His rank as Colonel demanded automatic respect, making his race irrelevant.

The day after my father's return, we went to get the Morris, the first of the many automobile enterprises in which I was to accompany my father. He had never treated me as a child, and now that I was older, I became his partner. Our first joint venture was to get the car running.

Uncle Israel was a shambling figure, who wore a variety of old tweed suits that looked as if he slept in them. He had the Cohen trademark, pure white hair, uncombed and adding to his disheveled appearance. He was the kind of man who never noticed that I had carefully combed my own hair, and he'd greet me affectionately by ruffling my hair, making me grimace. He was a man without guile and anyone could see the warm and generous heart behind his gruff manner.

We started to pull open the doors of Israel's stable, but they wouldn't budge.

'They're stuck!' I said.

'Of course they're bloody stuck!' said Uncle Israel. 'They haven't bloody been opened for four years!'

Bloody was Uncle Israel's favorite word. We pulled and pulled, and eventually with a loud groan, the doors did open. Inside it was quite dark, but there was enough light to see that the Morris was in a sorry state. My father looked at it in dismay and then his face took on that determined look again.

The car was covered in dust, the tires were flat, and so was the battery. My father had anticipated that and had brought a spare battery borrowed from another of my uncles. He took his jacket off, opened the car's hood and soon had the new battery hooked up.

Meanwhile, Uncle Israel and I were taking turns on a foot pump for the tires. Miraculously, they hadn't rotted. My father removed the spark plugs from the engine and started to clean them. I was impressed again: he seemed to know a lot about cars.

'Could do with some new plugs,' he said.

'You'll be lucky!' said Israel. 'You can't get bloody plugs, Ken, not even bloody black market ones.'

There was a tense moment as my father got into the driving seat, pulled out the choke knob, and then pulled on the starter knob. The engine turned over feebly, and just when we were despairing that it would ever start, it suddenly caught with a bang, blowing a big cloud of dark smoke out of the exhaust pipe. My father laughed with pleasure; he was motoring again!

'Your dad!' said Israel. 'He's got the luck of the bloody Irish!' Of course, Irish Canadian is what Israel thought he was.

My father drove out of the stable, into the cobble stone yard, and all three of us set to washing the car. It quickly came up with a surprising shine, apparently untarnished by its four year incarceration, and we set off jubilantly to take my mother out for a celebration lunch.

As we drove to Thirlmere Street, I could see that being behind the wheel again fired up my father's optimism. A car, even that old Morris, had a symbolic value for him that I couldn't know at that time; once more, he had become a driver, not black or white, just a man with a car, back in control of where and when he went. There may have been no tires or spark plugs or batteries available, but he had beaten the system and slipped back once more into his civilian disguise.

He had survived the war, he was in robust good health, he had re-united with his wife, and he was delighted with his quite grown-up son. He was sixty years old, but he had all the vigor and enthusiasm of a young man, and now he was sure that nothing was going to keep him from having a great life.

But getting the old Morris started was merely the beginning of the problems of running a car in post-war Britain. The next problem was gasoline. It was strictly rationed and had a red dye in it, and anyone entitled to a privileged extra ration, say a doctor, who was caught selling his 'red petrol', would face severe penalties. *[34]*

But my mother's family, the Cohens, had always lived on their wits, the whole clan were experts at getting things you couldn't get, and what they got for my father was Petrol Ration Books, so that he could buy gas at any station.

Most staple foods had been rationed during the war, including meat and all dairy products. Eggs had almost become a delicacy. But the Cohens discovered that black market eggs could be bought for a fairly hefty price from small farms on the Yorkshire Moors, the Bronte country.

For most people that information wouldn't have been of much use, because there were no buses or trains to those remote farms. But my father had his Morris, his dodgy Petrol Ration Books, and we made regular food-buying journeys.

I loved those trips into the Yorkshire hills and dales. We drove up there in the dead of the very cold winter of 1945, wrapped in blankets – the Morris had no heater – as my father skilfully threaded the small old car up the narrow, twisting lanes into the hills. We saw hardly any other cars, and when we reached the top of the hills, the view of the snow-covered Yorkshire Moors was spectacular, unchanged from when the Brontes wrote their novels there. There was a strong, chill wind, snowdrifts on the edges of the road and flurries of snowflakes straining the single windshield wiper.

When I read *Wuthering Heights* years later, the landscape it described conjured up more than Heathcliff for me.

As we drove, I listened in rapt attention as my father told us stories of his life in Iraq and India.

'Sometimes there were periods when we didn't have all that much to do, and I would take my soldiers to see the local sights. In the hills outside Bangalore, there was a monastery and one day the monks invited us to lunch.

'I took about twenty of the men with me, and it was about an hour's drive into the hills. The monks welcomed us warmly, but the head of the monastery asked to speak to me privately.

'Is one of your soldiers from the city of Sheffield?' he asked me.

I knew my men pretty well after two years and I told him, yes, one man was from Sheffield. 'How do you know that?' I asked him.

'I'm afraid I have bad news for that soldier,' said the

monk. 'I am sorry to tell you that his mother died this morning, while you were driving here.'

My father asked him, 'Do you have a telephone in the monastery?'

The monk shook his head, my father said, 'Then how do you know this?'

My father paused dramatically. My mother and I waited for the answer. He continued, 'The monk said, We know these things, Colonel.'

I asked him again, 'How do you know?'

He replied, 'There is more to life than you can touch and see, Colonel. Will you tell your soldier about his mother?'

I jumped in, 'Did you tell him, Dad?'

'No. I didn't believe the monk, and I didn't want to upset the soldier for no reason.'

Even my mother was impressed by this story. 'So what happened?' she asked.

My father spoke slowly. 'When we got back to the camp, late in the evening, there was an official telegram for me, informing me that the soldier's mother had died during the day.'

She asked, 'But how could the monk know that about it with no telephone?'

'It was magic!' I said. 'Wasn't it, Dad?'

'I don't know, son,' he said. 'There are some things that can't be explained.' He smiled a mysterious smile. 'Anyway, here's the farm.'

He turned the car in through the farm gate.

'I still think it was magic,' I said, looking at my mother.

'Don't be silly, Francis!' she said. And then laughed. 'Is that really a true story, Ken?'

'Oh, yes,' he said, getting out of the car, nodding seriously.

He left me and my mother sitting in the car with the motor running to keep us warm, while he went into the farmhouse and bought the black market foods. Was the story true? Or had he invented whole thing? I now know that he certainly had a flair for invention.

*

These trips were a chore for my mother, but they were exciting for me. I knew there was something illegal about them, and I loved the sense I got that my father was an adventurous person. For him those trips were an opportunity to break the rules and beat the system again, to break free from the restrictions he had imposed on himself.

I was just beginning to understand that he was a man who enjoyed getting away with something he shouldn't have. I'm sure those eggs tasted better to him than any we might have bought in a store.

Back in Thirlmere Street, my mother renewed the Cohen family tradition of Sunday afternoon tea – sandwiches and Jewish cookies she baked herself. My grandmother had presided over these gatherings of the whole clan, but now mother replaced her, and although she was the youngest of her siblings, it was the beginning of a process in which she became the matriarch of the family.

Once again, the old house was filled with uncles and aunts, and lots of children, mostly older than I was. But they all knew that it was only a matter of time before those gatherings came to an end, before we returned to London, to pick up our old life, in however different a form. It was the end of an era.

*

19 London Again!

In the summer of 1946, I said goodbye to yet another group of school friends. The Morris was jammed with everything we owned, spare cans of gas were tied to the roof, and we set off for a new life in London. For the second time.

The gasoline rationing ensured empty roads, and even with the mediocre performance of the Morris, we made good time.

Just north of Birmingham, we drove down a long unusually straight section of road, into the last of the afternoon sun. 'This is a Roman road,' said my father. 'If you're on any straight road in this country, you can bet the Romans built it. Any damn road that's full of twists and turns – and you can be just as sure the English built it!'

Then he glanced in the mirror and frowned. I turned to look back, to see what he had seen. A few hundred yards behind us, a car was slowly catching up with us. I heard the Morris's engine note change and felt the car slowly gather speed. We had been doing about 45 mph, a comfortable cruising speed for the small old car, but my father's foot was now flat to the floor, and his face had taken on a determined expression.

As we approached the giddy speed of 50 mph, the Morris was beginning to buzz and vibrate. My mother, who had been dozing, suddenly woke up and paid attention.

'What are you doing Ken?' she asked. He said nothing, shooting a quick glance in the mirror, his face grim.

I looked around, my mother looked around too.

Through the rear window we could now see that the car behind was definitely gaining on us. I prided myself on being able to recognize every make of car on the road, and I could now identify our pursuer as a Riley, a high performance make of the pre-war era.

I knew, as my father must have known, that the Morris could never be a match for it. We all sat there, feeling the vibrations increase as the Morris's speedometer began waving and fluttering towards 55 mph. Then, as it held steady, refusing to add even one more mph, the Riley closed to within a few yards.

'Slow down, Ken! We're not in a hurry!'

'God damn it, Sally, I'm *not* going to let him pass us!'

But the Riley could not be denied. At what seemed like a few inches at a time, it crept alongside. For a few moments we hurtled down the road as if bolted together, then the driver of the Riley, a cheerful, middle-aged man, looked directly across at us and smiled a friendly smile, which my father returned with a nod through gritted teeth.

Then, inexorably, the Riley drew ahead. My father reluctantly lifted his foot. 'Engine's getting a bit hot,' he said. The Morris slowly lost speed. Ahead of us, the Riley was beginning to disappear. My mother looked relieved, and leaned back in her seat again.

My father relaxed too, or perhaps he slumped. I saw that he had suffered some sort of a defeat, that it had temporarily dented his bright spirits and optimism. Had he for a moment become a second class citizen again? I hated to see my father beaten. I looked out of the window to avoid catching his eye.

Decades later, as I owned a series of Porsches and

Lotuses and Mercedes and Jaguars, I often thought back to that contest with the Riley, and I was never overtaken.

*

When we got back to East Ham, it was my mother who negotiated with the War Damage Commission to determine the amount of government compensation we would receive for the German bombing of the office. It was also my mother who went to the bank and got a loan, so that we could buy a storefront property, only a few yards from the building that been destroyed.

Without either of us knowing it, I was getting a lesson in feminism; I grew up with a healthy image of the role of a woman in a relationship.

Apart from the effects of the bombing, seen in the many vacant lots where houses and shops had been, East Ham was completely unchanged from 1939. But I had seen a lot more of England in the past six years and I was now conscious that it was an unvaried working class neighborhood, with a population consisting almost entirely of factory workers and dockers.

Before my father could open his office for business, the new storefront had to be altered to make it work both as a doctor's office, and as our home. This involved knocking down some walls, putting doors in other walls, and eventually building a garage, man's work. The building company was my father – and me. At the time, I took it as a matter of course that my father knew a great deal about building. He knew which walls you could remove without weakening the structure and I thought that all educated adults knew these things. But he had must have done some construction work at some time in his life, he knew how to do this stuff

As far as I know, without getting any kind of building permit, he just went ahead and converted the store-front to suit his purpose. London was trying to re-build everywhere and officials weren't looking too closely at what was done, they were simply pleased that a building was being refurbished.

Our first task was to create a doorway in an existing brick wall. While my father knocked a hole in the wall with a sledge hammer, I collected the broken bricks and debris and put it all in a wheelbarrow, which I then tipped outside on a vacant lot at the back of the house. I was ten and proud that I was able to manage the heavy wheelbarrow. I was astonished how quickly we created the doorway, and then impressed at how quickly my father framed it. I helped him to chisel out the wooden door frame from a doorway we were blocking up, and then we used that frame and its door in the new doorway.

As he worked and I watched or swept the floor, I learned a lot, mostly not to be intimidated by any kind of building work. The only awkward moment between us was when he sent me to fetch a particular pair of pliers and I came back saying I couldn't find it.

'Now, son,' he said, 'I know it's there, you didn't look properly.'

'Yes, but – ' I started.

He silenced me with a look. 'Francis,' he said, 'don't make me go and get it myself.'

I scuttled away to try again, anxious not to provoke

his wrath, but more anxious to retain his respect. He was right, I hadn't looked properly, and when I gave him the pliers a moment later, I was rewarded with a broad smile.

'Be thorough, man,' he said. 'If you're going to do something, do it thoroughly.'

I smiled back; I had passed some kind of test.

In remarkably few days, we had finished all the alterations, and although of course my father had done almost of all the real work, I felt a tremendous sense of shared accomplishment. Yet again, my admiration had increased, I felt very close to him.

Later, when I started to make model airplanes, our roles were reversed, as he became my helper. One day, he had good news for me: he had discovered a place called Fairlop, where we could fly the planes.

During the First World War many new airfields had been built on the eastern side of England to shorten the flying distance for the British reconnaissance and bomber planes on their missions to attack the German forces in France. Fairlop was one of those fields. After 1918, it became a flying club, but then in 1940, it was taken over by the RAF, and used as a base for many of the Spitfires that fought in the Battle of Britain. When that war ended, Fairlop was no longer needed and it was simply abandoned and left open.

A couple of weeks after my father told me about Fairlop, we drove out to the old airfield with a model I had worked hard on for six weeks. It was a control-liner, an aerobatic, gas-powered plane, controlled by the operator as it flew around him in a circle, on the end of a line with a handle that controlled the ailerons.

I was the pilot and my father was in charge of the

launch, but we had a misunderstanding about the settings of the ailerons. He fired up the engine, I moved back to tighten the control wires and shouted to him to let go. But he had pushed the ailerons too far in one direction and they had stuck in that position. The plane took off – and shot upwards in a almost vertical climb. I tried desperately to level it out, but within a second it had completed a loop and plowed back vertically into the tarmac.

Stunned, we walked across to the pile of balsa wood. My father examined the little motor. 'Crankshaft's bent,' he said glumly. I could see that he was more upset than I was and I tried to reassure him. 'The controls got stuck,' I said.

He said, 'I know, I stuck them!'

Driving back home, he asked me if I could face building another plane. I said I could.

'Then I'll get you another engine and another plane kit,' he said. 'But I think we better not tell your mother about this!'

I nodded, we were conspirators.

*

My father's caring nature, his highly intuitive diagnostic abilities, his eager investigation of new drugs and technologies, made him a highly effective doctor and a popular person in East Ham. He knew and was loved by all the families on his patient List; he knew about their jobs, about their family feuds, their career prospects and of course, their medical history.

There were few educated people in East Ham, and

so my father's patients, as well as getting his medical advice, would bring their job or pension applications for him to fill in. He played a role in the community somewhat like an old-fashioned parish priest.

Over thirty years after his death, I received a touching letter from the son of one of his patients, a man who had seen my name in the credits of a tv show I had directed, and who had written to me on the off chance that I was Dr. Megahy's son:

I still live in East Ham, he wrote, *and I am now a pensioner myself, but your surname evoked memories of Dr Megahy's great kindness to my father, who had many years of illness and was often out of work. Knowing of our hard circumstances, the doctor and Mrs Megahy often helped out with jobs and genuine help.*

I remember him as being a quiet, handsome and dignified man, and very caring. Mrs Megahy was a tiny vivacious lady, who seemed to totter about on very high heels.

Your name brought back warm memories of a very special couple.

John Elliott

*

When we returned to East Ham, I was ten, and now old enough, when I wasn't in school, to ride along with my father as he made house calls to sick patients. For both of us, it was a special time to be together. He'd give me the list of houses he had to visit and a map, and I would work out the best route. When he came out of each house, I'd tell him where we had to go next and he would tell me what was the medical problem of the patient he just had treated. I felt that I was making a contribution to his work.

He routinely complained about making the house calls, but I eventually came to see that he liked them. He liked helping his patients, solving their problems, and he was unusually aware that many of those problems were not essentially medical. This was back in the late 1940's, when it was highly unlikely that your illness would be identified by a British National Health Service doctor as the result of family, work or business stress. But for my father, psychological factors were a commonplace explanation of ailments.

One fall day in 1950, we stopped at a junction to let an older man on a bicycle ride cross in front of us. He and my father exchanged waves. My father told me, 'There's old Mr Jenkins, he's just retired from the Ford production line in Dagenham. My guess is that he'll probably be dead in for or five years.'

I asked what was wrong with Mr Jenkins and my father said, 'Nothing's wrong with him at the moment, but now he's given up his job he'll lose his identity and his dignity, and then slowly, his will to live. Then he'll get sick. He'll die of heart failure or some other disease, but that won't be the real reason. That's a pattern around here.'

My father gave me this explanation in such a matter-of-fact way that I had no idea how much it contradicted the conventional medical wisdom of the time.

We spent hours together, driving from one 'two-up-two-down' house in East Ham to another, talking about his patients and medical science, and of course, always about cars. We laughed together a great deal; shared laughter with my mother didn't exist then, and it took me years after my father's death to find a way to laugh with her.

Nevertheless, life at home again settled into a comfortable pattern. In the evening after dinner, my mother and I would listen to the radio, to plays and comedy shows, but there was also a lot of reading. My mother loved romance novels and the newspapers that were somewhere in between broadsheets and tabloids. My father read every issue of *The British Medical Journal* and *The Lancet*, but he also liked Western and thriller novels. One of my parents' great unconscious gifts to me was the image I have in my mind of them sitting and reading. Reading, books, magazines and newspapers, whether printed or on a tablet, has always been the way I have discovered the world.

In the late 1940's and early 50's, Britain might have been suffering from 'Austerity' and shortages and ration books, but it was a period of relative calm and stability. Our family life reflected the feeling in the country. Nobody had any idea that just around the corner lay the so-called social revolution of the 60's, which was to tear apart the fabric of the community. Society was less fluid then than it is now, and everyone knew their place, and even if they didn't like it, they more or less accepted it anyway.

This was a time when school teachers and doctors were still respected rather than suspected, but among the big changes that had come with the post-war left-wing governments was the introduction of The National Health Service. My father was an enthusiastic proponent of it.

He took his medical practice took very seriously on every level. As well as his extensive reading about new pharmaceutical and surgical developments, every couple of weeks or so, he'd be out for the evening at a lecture or seminar. I would hear him complain when he got home that there were thirty-seven doctors in his area of the National Health Service and, 'Not one of them was there tonight. Those old duffers are still prescribing the drugs they learned about in medical school thirty years ago!'

This was when he was already over sixty, so most of the 'old duffers' were actually much younger than he was. But one of the qualities he shared with my mother was his incredible energy, not the fizzing, fidgeting kind: he could sit in his favorite armchair and read for hours. But until he was in his mid-seventies, I simply cannot recall him ever being tired. And right up to the day he died, he was available out of hours for his patients, and would get up in the middle of the night to attend to them.

Then, as now, working class pensioners struggled to live on their meager retirement money, and since old people naturally tend to be sick, many of my father's patients fell into that category. Every Christmas my father would take my mother on a special shopping trip to the local Jewish grocers, where she would buy thirty or more small chickens and some other food supplies. Back at home, I would be enlisted to help as all three of us wrapped the chickens and the canned food and the rest of it into separate food parcels. It was then my chore to deliver these parcels to the old pensioners whom my father knew were having the hardest struggle and facing the bleakest Christmas.

Trudging through the chilly and grimy streets, this seemed like a tedious task, until a house door would open and a patient's face would light up at the sight of my parents' gift. I often wondered if any of them noticed that they were eating kosher food!

Driving or walking, Dr Megahy was a familiar figure on the streets of East Ham. Summer and winter he wore a felt hat, a mark of his generation and also of his experience of North American winters and summers.

'You lose forty per cent of your body heat through your head in the winter, son!' he would tell me, 'and the brain doesn't like to get hot, so you should wear a hat in the summer as well.'

But in a largely hatless society, his headgear marked him out, contributing to his slightly 'foreign' look. I feel sure that people in East Ham didn't for a second think he was English. For a start, they knew that he was Jewish, some of them even called him 'The Jewish Doctor'! And then there was the strange surname, which I doubt any of them knew was Scottish in origin, and there was also his voice. He had spent almost forty years away from the Caribbean and the years in North America had left their mark: his accent had US overtones that had pretty well obliterated its Barbadian cadences, and he still retained some of his American vocabulary, for example, always calling the garden 'the back yard'.

He invariably wore American shoes from the Walkover company in Oxford Street in the West End, and although I'm sure that nobody would have noticed that detail, he made a generally 'American' impression.

Black people of any kind were a rare sight in the

East End of the 1940's and the only dark-skinned people the community had regular contact with were Lascars, the almost blue-hued black Indian sailors who sometimes strayed from the hostels near the docks where their ships were temporarily berthed. But nobody seeing those skinny men in their flapping cotton shirts and trousers, shuffling along to keep their heel-less shoes on their feet, could have imagined that Dr Megahy had any racial connection to them. If anyone was pressed to guess my father's origins, looking at his olive skin tone, I think they might have said Greek, or perhaps Egyptian. Many of them undoubtedly thought he was American.

Africa would have been the last place anyone would have connected him to, so his secret was never betrayed by his appearance. This was just as well, because the people of East Ham were scarcely broad-minded, and if they had thought that Dr Megahy was what they called a 'Blackie', his welcome in the community might have been very different.

*

20 The Closet Rebel

My father and I didn't relate to each other through sports or any other physical activity. He played no sports and had no interest in them. The only sport I was interested in was motor racing. Unlike my mother, he never showed any interest in politics.

I was already developing my own lifelong interest in politics, and like my mother, I tended to support the underdog, the side of the working class, but nonetheless, I always felt much closer to my father than to her. She was the disciplinarian about religion, insisting that I go to *schul* on the Jewish holy days, which I detested. The services meant nothing to me and I didn't feel Jewish enough to identify with the congregation: I felt that I was in a room full of strangers performing a bizarre and meaningless ritual that was nothing to do with me.

My mother wasn't devout, but she was 'observant'; for almost all of her life she kept to the Orthodox Jewish dietary rules and lit the Sabbath candles every Friday evening. I knew that on the matter of religion, her mind was closed; we never talked about being Jewish. We just *were* Jewish; what was there to talk about?

I always knew that my father was a Jewish convert, and it was clear to me that he had no interest in religion at all, and by this stage in his life he wasn't even making much of an effort to pretend otherwise. He always managed to avoid the religious holidays; he somehow always found himself too busy attending to a particularly sick patient to make it to any of the services, and the only time I recall him in *schul* was either at family weddings or funerals in Manchester. In the Hightown ghetto, everyone had seemed to be Jewish. Where we lived in London, hardly anybody was. I felt alienated from the community around us and I consciously didn't want to be Jewish, I didn't want to be an outsider; I resisted any identification with the Jewish community.

As my Barmitzvah approached, I began to dread it more and more. Unlike most Jewish boys, I could get no help from my father and I disliked the miserable, authoritarian old men who taught in Hebrew School on Sundays. I resented giving up part of my weekend to it, and before the day arrived, I was already rehearsing in my mind the speech I would make to my mother after the ceremony: 'If I am now a man, my first decision as a man is no more religious services!'

Somehow, propped up by the rabbi, and a friend of the family who stepped in to save me each time I dried up, I struggled through to the end of my portion of the Talmud. It was a feeble, faltering performance and after it, I went home with my parents feeling a mixture of depression at my public failure and a feeling of elation that I would never have to do it again. I never did find the courage to make my prepared speech to my mother; I drew even closer to my father and more distant from her.

*

However, from my mother I inherited something of her mercurial character, her love of laughter and jokes and quick remarks that captured a moment with humor.

My father was not blessed with her talent for the rapid riposte, the quick comeback that can reduce a dining table full of friends to helpless laughter, not simply at the wit of the wit, but at the speed of it. I do have this quality, and it's a dangerous one, which has often worked to my detriment, when, infuriated by someone, I have instantly summoned a cutting remark, which a moment's reflection would have shown would have been better left unsaid.

My father didn't have that problem: he effortlessly kept his own counsel, felt no discernible need to burden others with his opinions, or indeed to impose himself on others in any way.

He was as adept at sustaining his smiling silence as he was adroit at deflecting all personal enquiries, so that after a quarter of a century of intimate contact with him, I found that I not only knew almost nothing about him – I didn't even know how little I knew.

It wasn't until after his death that I realized what a clever, witty and resourceful woman my mother was. Educationally, I had more in common with my father, and found it much easier to talk to him. My mother made emotional leaps in conversation that I found very frustrating; like my father, I tended to think analytically. But however much I had in common with him, the range of things we never talked about was extraordinary: never about his parents, never about his own youth, or his experiences in the US.

*

I was learning from my father all the time, but he was such a subtle man, that I didn't know it was happening. When I was just sixteen, with two friends from school, I went on a cycling holiday to France, to Brittany. My mother was reluctantly persuaded to agree to this trip and didn't disguise her anxiety about it.

'Now, sonny, don't do anything dumb,' my father whispered as I prepared to leave. 'I'm relying on you to be sensible – because your mother will never forgive me if something happens to you!'

We exchanged our private smiles and I pedaled away.

Apart from running out of money and spending a night sleeping in a farmer's field and being woken by a dog licking my face, the holiday was uneventful. But all that cycling had shown me a number of inadequacies in my bicycle, and when I got back, I asked my father if he'd buy me a better one, which I knew he could afford. I knew exactly which bicycle I wanted, a handmade racing bicycle, a Stallard. I had read about Percy Stallard, the man who had stood up to the bicycling establishment to bring street cycle racing to Britain. Stallard was a rebel and I saw his bicycles as a symbol of his independent nature.

There were still two months left of my very long school summer holiday. My father said, 'Here's the deal. You work all the rest of the summer, save up as much money as you can, and then before you go back to school, we'll talk about it again.'

I said, 'Work? What at?'

'That's up to you!'

In Britain, unlike America, young people don't work in their vacations, and my father's proposition was revolutionary, and baffled my school friends.

'Couldn't he just buy you the bicycle?' asked David Ross.

I shrugged, I thought he could have; maybe I was wrong. It was the beginning of a series of horrible summer jobs: I worked as a house painter's laborer, I worked on the sock counter of Selfridges department store in London's West End, and then as a ticket clerk for a bus company. I slogged through the summer, finishing at the bus company just a few days before I had to go back to school.

I'd been counting up my money every week, and in the end I had less than a third of the cost of the bicycle. Over dinner with my parents, just when I was trying to think up a strategy for convincing my father to put up the rest of the cost of it, he asked, 'So how much have you saved?' With some trepidation, I told him. He nodded and smiled at my mother. 'That's not too bad, is it, Sally?' he said. He turned to me and said, 'We'll go to the bicycle store tomorrow and see what they have.'

To my amazement, what they had was the Stallard, which my father had ordered a couple of weeks before. I was thrilled.

'I knew you'd do all right,' he said. 'You stuck to it – that's the most important thing.'

Without any discussion of principle, my father had taught me a lifelong lesson about the relationship between effort and reward, and about the value of perseverance. Two days later, I rode my Stallard to school, feeling exceptionally strong and confident.

*

Later in the year, when I was still sixteen, a year younger than the legal minimum age for driving a car, I could scarcely contain my excitement when he suggested that he would teach me to drive. He had decided that Fairlop, the old wartime airfield, would be the ideal safe place for my illegal, under-age driving lessons.

In the years immediately after the war, new cars were virtually unobtainable, and my father was still driving our 1935 Morris 8 and so this was the car I learned to drive on the abandoned runways and perimeter roads. Although it only had a 3-speed stick shift and rather less power than a modern ride-on lawn-mower, it was an incredible thrill when I learned to start, stop, shift gears and steer smoothly. Once I had acquired those skills, my father occasionally allowed me to drive him at night on the public streets, and sometimes at weekends I drove both him and my mother on quiet country roads.

As I approached seventeen, the minimum legal age for driving in Britain, I had driven with him many times, and one Monday evening when my mother was getting ready to go out to her weekly card game, I was in our small sitting room, behind his office, with my father. I was reading a model airplane magazine and he was deep into a paperback thriller when the door opened and my mother said, 'I'm ready, Ken.'

Without looking up, he said, 'Just let me finish this page.'

I read her impatient look and said quickly, 'I'll drive you.'

'Like hell you will!' she said.

My father looked up, slowly glancing from one of

us to the other, and then he said, 'Why not? You know he can drive, Sally.' As he reached in his pocket for the car keys, she said, 'Are you mad!'

He gave me a very serious look and said, 'Now, son, I'm trusting you not to do anything silly, because if you get caught driving I could lose my license. All right?'

The room stood still for a moment and I thought my mother was going to explode, but to my amazement she just turned and walked away toward the front door. Excitedly, I took the car keys from my father as my mother called out, 'Well, come on!'

As we drove through then-deserted streets of East London, she told me, 'Now don't drive fast, Francis, whatever you do!' and then, 'Your father's got no sense, you know that, don't you!'

It didn't even cross my mind that she was showing at least as much trust in me as my father had.

When I got back to the house, he was still reading. He hardly looked up as I walked in and asked me, entirely casual, 'Everything all right?'

I said, 'Yes. Yes, fine.'

I handed him the car keys and he went back to his book, apparently unconcerned, but I thought that I caught him giving himself the very slightest nod of satisfaction.

I was proud that he trusted me, and after that evening I drove my mother to her card game every week. She accepted the arrangement but I always thought that she took her seat in the car with some apprehension. I still remember my sense of excitement each Monday evening when she got out and I was free and in sole charge of the car for the drive home, at a somewhat higher speed!

Although I never took it seriously at the time, the recklessness of my father's behavior in allowing me to drive the car seems totally at odds with what I always understood as his conservative character, because he was placing us both in some serious legal jeopardy. If the police had caught me driving his car, he would have lost his license, no trivial matter for a doctor, for allowing it to be driven by someone unlicensed, who was therefore not insured. The sole alternative would have been for me to say that I had taken it without his permission, which would have resulted in the police charging me with car theft.

The only explanation that makes any sense of the whole episode is that I had a fundamental misunderstanding of him, that there was a hidden, reckless side to him that I never recognized. Of course, he took this risk in his usual quiet way, not getting excited or raising his voice. But he obviously got some kind of a kick out of it. And I now see that the trust he placed in me was one of the many ways that he used his relationship with me to develop my self-confidence.

The sketchy outlines I knew of his early life, which were substantially correct, certainly suggested a man with a taste for low-key adventure; he'd worked around the Caribbean, worked in the US, changed his entire life when he moved to Britain, and enjoyed his military service in World War Two. But when I knew him, he was buttoned down in so much of his life, that I believe the adventurous side of his nature had to burst out somewhere.

I have another memory of the reckless side of him.

East Ham was not only the home of respectable working class people, it also harbored a good number of criminals. The docks were a fruitful source of theft opportunities, and it was in East Ham that I first heard the expression 'it fell off the back of a truck'. My father might mention to me occasionally that 'Mrs Smith's youngest son' was back 'inside', and the fact of crime and criminals was a commonplace in the community. I recall that there was one family that seemed to engage in little but criminal activity, the Jamiesons.

Late one night, after we had all gone to bed, there was a ring at our doorbell, and for some reason it was insistent enough to wake me. I lay in bed half-asleep, and heard my father open the front door, and then men's voices, rough and with an anxious tone. I couldn't distinguish any words, but I could hear some hesitation in my father's voice, and finally I did hear him say clearly, 'All right, you better come in.' Then I heard the men come into the building and go into my father's office.

I drifted off to sleep, but I was woken again by the sound of the men leaving. I heard my father walking back upstairs and as he reached his bedroom, I heard my mother asking him what had happened and I clearly heard his reply. 'One of the Jamieson boys got himself shot,' my father said, 'and I took the bullet out for him.' As the door closed again, I heard my mother protesting that this was crazy. The last thing I heard was my father saying, 'Well, it's done now.'

Obviously, the 'Jamieson boy' had got himself shot in the perpetration of a crime of some sort, and what my father had done was seriously illegal, for which the penalties would be much harsher than losing his driver's license. In the morning, I remembered the incident and said to my mother over breakfast, 'Did some patients come around late last night?'

She gave me a hard look and said, 'You've got too much imagination, that's your trouble!'

I looked at my father, who gave the merest shrug: I don't know what you're talking about. We never spoke of this incident again.

I now wonder if perhaps, amidst the deception required to maintain his racial secret, which I might have thought was an insufferable burden, he had discovered a way to get some satisfaction; letting his under-age son drive his car illegally one night a week, taking a bullet out of a wounded gangster, these were acts of rebellion that maybe restored some of the dignity which was daily damaged by his rejection of his own true self; and restored some self-esteem to the closet-rebel he had become.

*

21 My Father Takes A Trip: Chicago, NY, Trinidad

Three years after he returned from his service in World War Two, my father decided that it was time that he made a journey to visit his brother Evan in Chicago, and his half-brother Norman in Trinidad.

This time, unlike his war-time departure for the Middle East, we went to Southampton see him off on the *Queen Mary*, bound for New York.

In Southampton, there was a feeling of excitement when we were allowed onto the ship to say goodbye. I couldn't believe the size of it. Family was always the center of the world for my mother, and she was very pleased for my father, that he was going to see his brothers after such a long time, but I could see that her emotions were mixed. While he was away during the war, I had never thought about how each of them missed the other, only about myself.

We stood on the deck, and my mother said, 'I'll miss you, Ken.'

My father smiled, 'I know, I know you will,' he said.

I had never thought about the love between them, but as he hugged her before we had to leave the ship, in their physical reluctance to part I saw the strength of the feeling between them, perhaps for the very first time. I was going to miss him as well, but I was excited about his journey, and the ship, and the thought of America, that mythical country I was beginning to know so well through the movies. I said to him, 'It's not dangerous, on this ship, is it, Dad?'

He laughed cheerfully. 'Not at all, son,' he said, 'don't you give it a thought, man!'

But when the final moment came, he hugged me and pressed me to his chest, and as we moved apart I was astonished to see the tiniest tear in the corner of his eye.

'Take care of your mother, Francis,' he said. 'I'm counting on you, man!'

Standing on the dockside and watching the great liner slide from its berth, my mother suddenly put her arm around my shoulder, tight.

'Was Dad crying when we left?' I asked her.

'Your father? I don't think so!'

I looked up at her and I knew that we had both seen that small tear. 'It's only for a few weeks, Mum,' I said.

Now she took my arm and turned away, 'Come on,' she said. 'Time to catch our train!'

At the beginning of the train ride back to London, we were silent, and then I remembered that my father had hired a locum to fill in for him while he was away.

'How do you think the locum will be, Mum?' Staring out of the window, at the gray-green fields of Surrey rolling by, she looked tired, then gave me a tight smile, 'I'm sure we'll get along very well with him.'

*

The locum was an Austrian, a Displaced Person from World War Two, who had settled in Britain after the end of hostilities. He was a warm, charming man with a professorial look, and a shy manner. My mother had rented a room for him near my father's office, and in the evenings he joined us for dinner. I liked him, he was easily teased, and when I heard him coming I would open the door to our living room and announce loudly, 'Dr Otto Nemet, MD, Vienna!' After that, he always walked in laughing.

When the *Queen Mary* docked, my father didn't stay in New York, but immediately took another ship for Trinidad. There he found his half-brother healthy and prosperous, with a thriving medical practice, a fine home in Port of Spain, and a rural estate on the Rio Claro in Mayaro, some 30 miles south of the capital. My cousin Robert, named after my grandfather, was a newly-qualified dentist, and a world class shot. In fact, Norman and Robert took my father duck-hunting on a river on their Mayaro property. Robert was handsome, tall and light-skinned. His dentistry degree was from the US, and he and his father were part of the Trinidad upper class; their friends were judges and politicians.

Trinidad was a multi-racial society, much like Barbados, and my father felt perfectly at home there with his family. When he returned to the US, to Chicago, he found himself in a very different world.

It was almost twenty years since he had been in Chicago, and he must have wondered what developments had taken place in the meantime. He quickly found that there had been little if any easing of the tension between the races. 1948 was a particularly inauspicious year for him to visit; it was the year of the founding of the breakaway political party, the segregationist Dixiecrats.

Perhaps my father had been misled by reading President Truman's speech made the year before, in which he sounded a warning to the racist South that the Union was going to try and set its house straight:

It is my deep conviction that we have reached a turning point in the long history of our country's efforts to guarantee freedom and equality to all our citizens. Recent events in the United States and abroad have made us realize that it is more important today than ever before to insure that all Americans enjoy these rights.

And when I say all Americans — I mean <u>all</u> Americans.

The civil rights laws written in the early years of our republic, and the traditions which have been built upon them, are precious to us. Those laws were dawn up with the memory still fresh in men's minds of the tyranny of an absentee government. They were written to protect the citizen against any possible tyrannical act by the new government in this country.

But we cannot be content with a civil liberties program which emphasizes only the need of protection against the possibility of tyranny by the Government.

As Americans, we believe that every man should be free to live his life as he wishes. He should be limited only by his responsibility to his fellow countrymen. If this freedom is to be more than a dream, each man must be guaranteed equality of opportunity. The only limit to an American's achievement should be his ability, his industry and his character. The rewards for his effort should be determined only by these truly relevant qualities.

It was a fine speech and it is a shocking indictment that in the twenty-first century, its lofty aspirations have yet to be realized.

The Southern Democrats didn't like those

aspirations, and the last straw was when Hubert Humphrey declaimed at their Convention in 1948, '*To those who say, my friends, we are rushing this issue of civil rights, I say to them we are 172 years late! To those who say this civil-rights program is an infringement on states' rights, I say this: the time has arrived in America for the Democratic party to get out of the shadow of states' rights and walk forthrightly into the bright sunshine of human rights!*'

Many enraged Democrats walked out and held their own convention in Birmingham, Alabama. They nominated South Carolina Governor Strom Thurmond to head the new, disingenuously named, States' Rights Party, also known as the Dixiecrats.

Thurmond, who was famously quoted as saying '*All the laws of Washington and all the bayonets of the Army cannot force the Negro into our homes, into our schools, our churches and our places of recreation and amusement*', ran in the 1948 election on a blatantly racist platform: opposing the end of segregation in the US Army; opposing the right of black people to vote; opposing the right of black people to receive police protection from criminals such as the Ku Klux Klan – and supporting discrimination against black people in Federal hiring.

Thurmond came by his racism honestly: his father had been the campaign manager for 'Pitchfork' Ben Tillman, a virulent white supremacist who became Governor of South Carolina. Thurmond senior was instrumental in helping Tillman draft the nineteenth century laws that ensured legal segregation, and stripped the blacks of all political power in South Carolina.

So race was still a hot issue in the America my father had landed in – and the Dixiecrats tried to turn up the heat.

Fortunately, in the 1948 Election they failed. Predictably they won in Louisiana, Mississippi, Alabama, and South Carolina, but nationwide they got only 2.4% of the total vote. Eventually most of them became Republicans.

Adding to his failed bid to become a segregationist President, Strom Thurmond would later embellish his record of shame with his 1957 filibuster against Lyndon Johnson's Civil Rights Act. Thurmond spoke for a Senate record of 24 hours 18 minutes – but lost the vote. The final revelation of this world-class bigot's hypocrisy came after his death, when his illegitimate daughter stepped out of the shadows; she was a black woman, the result of his union with a black sixteen year old servant girl – a girl who worked in his family's house.

For my father, walking along Chicago's Michigan Avenue in the summer of 1948, the feeling in the city would hardly have been any different from walking along Michigan Avenue in the summer of 1916, but perhaps the failure of Thurmond and the Dixiecrats, and the impassioned speeches of Truman and Humphrey, encouraged my father to think that the US might be on a new course and he might find a new life again in the North East – with his racial past no longer a bar to a good life.

Chicago may have been little changed, but the brother that my father met was a very different man from when they had last seen each other. Now, Evan was the Treasurer of Illinois Savings and Loan, an S &

L he had helped to found. He was still the Junior City Engineer of the City of Chicago, he had become a medical doctor himself, and was altogether a very accomplished, prosperous and successful man.

But he had also helped to found something else, the American West Indian Association. Evan's partners in his S & L were all black, and all his friends were black. He had only one problem in his life: his son, my other cousin Robert, white-skinned and fair-haired, who was already set on the downward trajectory that would characterize the rest of his life.

This was all in sharp contrast to my father's life in Britain, where he had now successfully passed as white for almost a quarter of a century, where his wife was white, all his in-laws were white, his son was white, and where none of us knew anything of his real life story. The chasm between the brothers had widened.

The black area of Chicago's Michigan Avenue was redolent with reminders of the circumscribed life my father had managed to escape from so many years before. But when he got back to New York, and walked the streets of Manhattan, my father felt at home again, and felt that he might have a life in that city.

In New York, he met up with an old Army buddy, Jack Kaufman, a Jewish American veteran he had met in India. He received a warm welcome from his friend's white family, and Jack said that he hoped that my father would consider again living in the US.

Of course, when my father returned to us in East Ham, there could be no discussion of the 'racial' aspect of his holiday – but he was obviously invigorated by his trip. He brought wonderful presents: my favorite one was my 'American' suit, a fairly bright blue, double-breasted, real grown-up man's suit, of a kind simply not available in Britain in 1948 for a thirteen year old boy.

My mother and I saw immediately that the trip had re-kindled his interest in the US. He talked enthusiastically about the country, there was so much that he liked, the ease of travel, the feeling of boundless opportunity – he even liked the houses better, with their greater size and efficient central heating. The US was no longer the country he remembered from the Great Crash and the Depression, the war had revived American industry, and the country was heading for its post-war boom.

Despite the tensions with his brother and the continuing tense racial atmosphere in Chicago, he had a new belief that with his white wife and white son, he could live a successful life in the US, in the right place, and that meant in New York.

I began to overhear conversations between my parents about moving us to the US, where my father would earn much more money, and where there might be no Oxford or Cambridge for me, but there was certainly Harvard and Yale.

I'm not sure how strong was his desire to move back to the US, but I know that talk of it dismayed my mother.

She had grown accustomed to living in London; it was two hundred miles from her family, an easy train ride that she took every couple of months, but the thought of being separated from them by a ocean voyage – in those pre-jet days – of several weeks, well, that tested the limits of her worldview.

My father soon sensed that he would never convince her to make the move to the US, and he certainly didn't want to leave or break up his family, so after a while he accepted the status quo and we settled back into our previous routine. Once again, our evenings were spent listening to BBC Radio plays, reading, and for me, the construction of ever more complex model aircraft. I don't know what my father was thinking, but I recall it as a relaxed and tranquil period.

But even when he was buried in his medical magazines and pulp fiction, my father was always thinking, thinking in the long term, and he was formulating another of his plans: if he couldn't move to the US, he would create an American lifestyle in England.

*

In Trinidad, on the Myara river, duck-hunting in 1948: my cousin Robert Brewster; my father; an unknown domestic servant

Uncle Evan on the steps of the Savings and Loan he helped to found in Chicago; note his confrontational stance

The author at 13 wearing the Macy's suit my father brought back from New York in 1948

22 My Education

My cousin Robert had completed his high school education at Harrow, in London in the 1930's. I don't know what kind of rivalry my father had with his brother, but he was equally ambitious about my own education.

By the time a decision had to be made about which private high school I would attend, my father didn't want me to go the same school as my cousin Robert. My mother didn't want me to go to a boarding school, so that left the two pre-eminent London private day schools, Westminster and St Paul's. Both my father and his brother obviously knew that like everything else in Britain, education is deeply related to class, and one of the ways in which families have traditionally changed their class over one or two generations, is by sending their children to prestigious schools, where they will hopefully acquire the tastes, style and manner of the upper classes, as well as some versions of the three R's.

Up to this point, I had been attending East Ham Grammar school, which was scarcely a distinguished academic institution, and there was some doubt that I could pass the critical private school entrance examinations. My father decided to send me to a 'crammer', a coaching school designed to get the backward children of wealthy parents through those examinations.

The crammer was an interesting experience; it was in Kensington, an expensive neighborhood of a kind new to me. Walking around the neighborhood of the school, looking in through the windows of the white stucco houses, I saw antique furniture and paintings, a life style I had never seen before outside a movie theater. My fellow students were also an interesting bunch. One of them, Chris Deyong, was the first American I had ever met. He talked out of the side of his mouth, with a pronounced Brooklyn accent and had a cynical attitude beyond his years, which I admired and tried to emulate.

I'd repeat some received wisdom and with a twisted grin he'd ask, 'You really believe that?'

I learned not to answer. He wore a double breasted blazer and bow ties, and was a terrific table tennis player – I was most impressed.

Sending me to the crammer was a successful plan: after several interviews with me and my parents, the quaintly designated High Master of St Paul's agreed to admit me. Looking back I'm slightly surprised. I was of reasonably good academic quality, but in many ways I came from the wrong side of the tracks. My accent, always a key matter in Britain, had an unfashionable combination of Manchester and East Ham; my mother was noticeably of working-class origin and my father was obviously from Somewhere Else; and we still lived in East Ham. Also, we were Jews. However, although St. Paul's was originally affiliated with St. Paul's Cathedral and is a Christian school, it has a very liberal charter, forbidding it to discriminate against potential students on grounds of 'race or creed' – perhaps that's how I squeaked in.

My parents were both thrilled that I got into St Paul's, and the school did indeed change my life. Traveling there every day introduced me to the posh neighborhoods of London, and I made friends who were from an entirely different social class from anyone I had ever known, with very different lives. A number of my fellow students were the children of brilliant Jewish intellectual families, including the future neurologist, Oliver Sacks, and the future opera director, Jonathan Miller, but I found myself identifying as much with the main body of the students as with the minority of Jews.

I visited my friends' homes, and they visited mine. As much as I was fascinated by Hampstead and the other posh London areas they lived in, they were fascinated by East Ham, with its dimly-lit streets and overtones of East End gangsters. We went to dance halls like the Winter Hall and the Harmonic Hall, where, doing a dance known as The Creep, we could press our adolescent bodies up against the local girls in a way that my friends from the ritzier parts of town were quite unused to.

I was becoming distracted from my school work, and although I was quick and smart, I wasn't a great student. My father paid more attention to this than my mother, he was always the lead player in the conversations about my mediocre end-of-semester reports. He saw that I was developing an interest in the wider world, and if sometimes I did less well at school than my intelligence suggested I should, if he noted, for example, that I might be slipping behind in my reading of one of the books on the curriculum, such as Alexander Pope's poem *The Rape of the Lock*, he would ask me if I was reading anything else 'other than car magazines.' When I told him that I was reading Dickens, and planned to start on Dostoevsky and the great Russian novelists of the nineteenth century, he nodded, 'That's good, but don't neglect your school work. If you want to succeed in life, man, you got to succeed at school.' In his world, there was no informal success; he had got where he was through relentless hard study.

In class-conscious Britain, my father's efforts to move me up the social scale were succeeding, and my accent and my manner was gradually changing; private school kids spent a lot of time lounging around, and they stood and walked in a different way from the working class kids I'd been in school with in East Ham. How pleased both my father and mother must have been to see in their house their son's friends from the more upscale parts of London. If my friends had any response to my father's ethnicity, I knew nothing of it. Our family vacations were often driving trips to the West of England, and on one occasion we took my friend John Wood, later to become my lawyer and lifelong confidant, with us to Devon.

When I recently told John of my discoveries about my father, he said, 'Absolutely amazing! I remember him very well from when your parents took me on holiday with them. My mental picture is of a fit-looking, thin and tanned gentleman in a white panama jacket, and his features were not in the least African. He was, I remember, courteous and charming to me, which to a teenager was a rare attitude to meet in an adult.'

He thought for a moment and then added, 'Thank your stars that the fall of the genetic dice made you rather less black than I am [!], so that you never had to bear that huge weight of unspoken prejudice that I believe every black man and woman suffers throughout life.'

This prompted me to write to other friends who had known my father, to ask how they remembered him.

My friend Florin Aftalion once visited from Paris for a weekend, we stayed very late at a party in London, and he gave me a lift back to the family home in Chigwell and met my father over breakfast the next day. I wondered what he thought; he wrote to me:

Hi Francis!

I think I only met your father once. It was somewhere out of the city. Could you have driven me there? I don't recollect. I vaguely remember he had a black mustache. He looked very British to me.

Martin McKeand, who produced a couple of my best films, wrote:

I find the story about your black antecedents quite amazing! I do remember your father, though I think I only met him once when for some reason we drove out to Chigwell. I remember him as looking very tired and having a vaguely Anglo-Indian complexion, almost olive toned, but the features were semitic/caucasian, definitely not negroid.

My father was very friendly with our family dentist, John McLean, I called John in London and asked, 'What race do you think my father was?'

He sounded surprised. 'What *race*..? I don't know... I never thought about it.'

'Well, if you think about it now...?'

He paused. 'I suppose...he could have been Turkish, possibly... Egyptian. Maybe, at a push, Indian...but as I say, I never thought about it.'

*

23 Uncle Evan's Visit

A superficial description of my father and his brother would suggest that they were alike· they both had the same kind of childhood; went to the same schools in Barbados; both went to the US to study; both became doctors; and both had one child, a son, whom they sent to expensive London schools.

In fact, they couldn't have been more different. I never knew my paternal grandparents, but I can only assume that their children were so different temperamentally because one of them was like his father and the other like his mother. But the real difference was in the way these two men lived their lives.

One of the most significant insights into my father's life came when I investigated the life of my Uncle Evan. I hardly knew my uncle, and before I traced and met his family in Kalamazoo, my impression of him was based entirely on two things: a two-week holiday he spent in London fifty years ago, when I was seventeen; and his response to the news of my marriage, some sixteen years later.

When Evan came to visit us in 1952, it was our last summer in East Ham, just before my family moved to Chigwell. He and my father had only seen other once in the previous twenty-two years, when my father made the trip to see him in Chicago in 1948. Evan, who seemed to have plenty of money, stayed in the ritzy Park Lane Hotel in Piccadilly and made regular visits out to East Ham to see us.

He was a ruggedly-built man, with a barrel chest and a ramrod straight posture, the perfect physical embodiment of his confrontational temperament. He didn't walk, he strode, when he came in through a door, you had the feeling that he'd just kicked it open. His nose was more aquiline than my father's and his skin color was a little darker. But that's a judgement I now make from photographs. I have no recollection that at the time the color of his skin made any impression on me at all; the thought that Evan and my father had any ancestral connection with Africa wasn't then on even the periphery of my consciousness.

When Evan's son, my cousin Robert, was at Harrow, he stayed with my father in Manchester during the school holidays, and the whole Cohen clan got to know him and became fond of him, especially my mother.

This was before I was born, so I never knew him, but I recall my mother saying many times, 'Your cousin Robert had beautiful wavy hair and he was the most handsome young man I ever saw!' I had seen photographs of Robert during his stay in England and he was indeed a good-looking young man with a perfectly white skin.

I believe now that Robert must have been part of my father's deception of my mother and her family. Not only must he have met both his grandparents of mixed race when they were living on the Upper West Side, but when I checked the Ellis Island immigration records, there was a Ship's Manifest listing Uncle Evan returning from Barbados in 1921 with the eleven year old Robert. It's inconceivable that on this trip, Robert did not hear about the entire family history from his father; Robert must have been familiar with his own black ancestry. The risk that familiarity carried for my father was that when Robert came to England to study, any casual, natural remark he made could inadvertently have exposed my father.

The only way that my father could have protected himself against this was by telling his nephew that my mother and her family knew nothing of their roots in Barbados and instructing him never to mention it. But my father could have had a strong motive for introducing Robert to my mother and her family in Manchester: the fair-skinned appearance of his nephew would have further allayed any suspicions that any of them might conceivably have had about my father's race.

My parents were both very fond of Robert, but I don't think they had those same feelings about Evan; although my father was careful never to say anything negative about him, I always felt a ripple of hostility between the two brothers.

Certainly, Evan's persona was very different from my father's. If my father's low-key manner was designed to avoid drawing attention to himself, Evan's main aim was to get attention. He was aggressive, dictatorial and bombastic. Back in Chicago, with his job with the City, his medical practice, and his role as Treasurer of the bank, he was a wealthy and successful man.

On his one visit to London, I was assigned to be his driver, using my father's prized Sunbeam-Talbot. The trouble started as soon as Evan saw the car parked outside the hotel. He got in, making that maneuver as difficult as possible, and immediately started complaining, 'Why the hell did your father buy this little tin-can! Why didn't he get a car big enough for regular people!'

It was the beginning of a unpleasant week. I drove him around all the popular tourist sights: Westminster Abbey, the Houses of Parliament, St. Paul's cathedral, the Tower of London, and so on, and he found some problem with all of them.

'History is bunk!' he'd declare loudly, hoping to be heard by anybody who happened to be nearby. 'This is just another Goddamn pile of old stones. They should knock it all down it all and build some new stuff!'

Then he'd drag me into a pub for lunch. He'd order some sandwiches and beers, and rant and rave to the people behind the bar, or whatever unfortunate person who happened to be standing next to him, 'This beer is like warm piss! How can you people drink this crap! And these sandwiches, they're pathetic. You people need to come over to the States and taste some real, cold beer and see what a real sandwich tastes like!' Again and again I cringed.

Then we'd go into a bank to change some money. 'Why are we waiting so long? You need more Goddamn tellers in here!' he'd shout. 'Back home, I'm the Treasurer of a Bank, and I can tell you, we could teach you people how to run a bank!'

In retrospect, knowing what I know now, I have to think that he must have got some kind of incredible secret kick out of this behavior. At home in Chicago, where white Americans' knowledge and sensibilities were much more finely tuned to racial identification than anyone in Britain in the early fifties, he definitely wouldn't be mistaken for anything but a light-skinned black man, and I'm sure he could never have got away with taunting white people at random in this manner.

But in the London of that era, his race simply wasn't an issue. He was just a loudmouthed American.

He complained endlessly about my driving: 'Too Goddamn fast!' and the roads: 'Too Goddamn narrow!' and the traffic: 'Too Goddamn much of it!'

This all came to a head as we drove to the Maritime Museum in Greenwich. Thoroughly miserable in this tyrant's company, my concentration wandered, I took a wrong turn and we found ourselves mired in a one-way street, full of crawling traffic. He started to curse me, and I exploded, following my mother's oft-repeated advice: don't get stress – give it!

'I'm *not* your son!' I told him. 'I'm doing you a favor driving you around at all. I am *not* a chauffeur, and if you don't like the car or my driving, you can bloody well get out now and take a bus back to your hotel!'

To my amazement, this outburst stopped him dead in his tracks and revealed that he was not after all a tyrant, but merely a bully. Once I stood up to him, that was the end of the trouble. He smiled, 'All right, son, take it easy,' he said. 'Take it easy,' and during the rest of the afternoon he revealed a charm I couldn't have suspected lurking beneath his previously abrasive manner.

Even more surprising, we developed an understanding, which by the end of his holiday had developed into a kind of friendship. So much so that when I got married in 1968, six years after my father's death, and my mother wrote to tell Evan about my wedding, he sent me $3000 as a wedding gift, an extremely generous amount at the time, which was in fact the deposit on my first marital home in Primrose

Hill.

When Uncle Evan's vacation came to an end, I could see that my father had mixed feelings. I'm sure that he loved his brother, but he was thoroughly tired of being told that he was doing everything wrong in his life. My father was very happy with his family and his work and his life, and clearly didn't like being told that he lived in a lousy house and that he deserved better. Typically, he kept his own counsel and he was obstinate enough to feel no obligation to explain to his brother that he was building his dream house and that within months we would be moving into it. On the occasions when I saw my father and Evan together, I could see that my father was doing his best simply to tolerate him, knowing that each day brought the end of his visit nearer.

Ever since Robert's stay in England, Evan would have known about my father's fake identity, but I can only guess what he thought about it. The two brothers clearly shared similar ambitions for their sons, but at the time of Evan's visit I knew nothing of his life in Chicago, so it didn't occur to me that this might be a strategy to guarantee the brothers' sons unquestioned entree to white society.

I know now that Evan was very fond of Barbados, and continued to visit the island for the whole of his life, but looking back on the many family meals we ate with him, I recall lots of conversation about Chicago and the US, but not a word about my grandparents or Barbados or the family's struggles in New York. It's hard to imagine that my father and his brother never reminisced about some kind of 'old days', or their early lives, but if those conversations ever took place, it was not within earshot of me or my mother.

There was much more to the brothers' interaction than the obvious clash of their temperaments. Beneath the apparent, superficial conflict, I believe that there was a profound antagonism between them, an antagonism whose origin was in their racial heritage and their different responses to it. As with almost everything else in my father's life, race was a determining factor, and his relationship with his brother was no exception to that.

*

24 My Education – Two

Throughout my time at St Paul's we lived in East Ham, and during that entire period, my father was considering the next step in my education. On Sunday afternoons, my mother would often say, 'Let's go for a ride in the car,' and we'd set off on the virtually traffic-free roads for 'Afternoon Tea' at some distant tea-room. But gradually, a pattern to these journeys emerged: we often seemed to drive the sixty miles either to Oxford or to Cambridge.

We would cruise these two small cities, identify a suitable tea-room, and then my father would park the car and we would stroll through the colleges. He knew a lot about the history of both cities. In Cambridge, he even had an account at Blackwell's, generally thought of then as the best bookshop in the world. He must have got to know Cambridge, and even opened his Blackwell's account, a couple of decades earlier when he had his practice in nearby St. Neots. As far as I know, he had never worked in or near Oxford, so his knowledge of that city must have been pure research, part of his planning ahead.

It wasn't hard to work out that he was trying to sell me on becoming a student at one of these two universities. I'm sure that he thought that with my white skin, and St Paul's school and Oxford or Cambridge on my resume, the remote ghosts of his own Caribbean past would be finally exorcized. But this part of his strategy was to founder on the rocks of his own liberalism.

*

Like everyone who had lived through the Depression, my father had an intense recollection of mass unemployment, and his chief ambition for me was that I would always be able to make a living. There was never any question in his mind or my mother's that I would engage in one of the 'professions', but he never had any desire for me to become a doctor, always claiming – falsely – that he didn't like the work. The choice was therefore Accountancy or Law – my meager math skills, added to the image of accountancy as the world's most boring activity, brilliantly lampooned decades later by Monty Python, meant I was pushed in the direction of Law.

I already knew that I wanted to make films, but whenever I tried to confess that embarrassing ambition, both of my parents would tell me that I had to first get the qualifications to make a living, then at some unspecified later date I could indulge these fantasies.

In that era, before the existence of one single film school, making films did feel like an exotic and unreal way to spend your life and I was always worried that my ambition would be ridiculed, that Those Who Knew Better would point a derisory finger at me, and say, 'You? *You?* Oh no, you need to be somebody *special* to make films!'

It's been amusing for me to watch the transition into a world of $1,000 HD video cameras and laptop editing, a world in which so many young people have the patently erroneous belief that they are talented film-makers.

But my father was an excellent judge of character and he had shrewdly observed that I had an aptitude for performing and thought that there could be a different but still professional setting for my performances – if he could persuade me.

Since I had expressed some interest in studying law, he bought me the autobiography of Frank Smith, a working class boy who became one of the most brilliant trial lawyers of the twentieth century, a career that culminated in the House of Lords as Lord Birkenhead. In Smith's book, he described one of his first cases, in which he represented the insurance company that insured the city of Liverpool's buses. One of these buses had hit a fifteen year old boy, whose family sued the bus company.

The company, suspecting fraud, allowed the case to come to trial, and took a chance on the young Frank Smith to defend the suit.

Cross-examining the boy, Smith asked him about the injuries to his arm. 'Your right arm is injured, is that correct?'

'Yes, sir.'

'You have limited use of it now?'

'Yes, sir.'

'Would you show the court how high you can raise your arm?' asked the youthful barrister.

The boy raised his arm until it was parallel with the ground.

'I see,' said Smith. 'And how high could you raise it before the accident?'

The boy instantly raised his arm until his hand pointed at the roof. It was a spectacular victory for Frank Smith, which made him famous overnight. My father's present achieved the result he wanted –

reading the story convinced me that I wanted to be a barrister, a trial lawyer.

*

25 The American Dream – In Essex

By the time of Uncle Evan's visit, we had been living in East Ham for six years – and it seemed longer.

My mother constantly complained about the small, inconvenient kitchen she had to work in, and both of my parents were tired of living in a working class area, with its poor shopping and other amenities. We probably could have moved after a couple of years, but after my father realized that there was no possibility of convincing my mother to move to the US, he was determined that when we did move, we would live in a thoroughly modern house, like the houses he had seen on his visit to America.

He and my mother began looking at houses, and although they saw some that my mother would have been happy with, none of them were what my father had in mind. Eventually my mother was exasperated enough to tell him, 'You won't find exactly what you want, Ken, nobody ever does.'

His smiled and nodded, in his non-confrontational way, and said, 'I know.'

'Well, then!'

'So we'll have to build a house.'

'*Build* a house? How long is that going to take, why we can't we compromise, like everyone else has to!'

This became a long, drawn-out conversation over several weeks. I was very enthusiastic about the New House Plan, because I was already very interested in architecture, and had some ideas of my own I was hoping to incorporate.

After a couple of months of unsuccessful house-hunting, my mother relented – my father could build his new house. They began searching for a suitable plot of land, somewhere attractive, affordable and within commuting distance of East Ham.

After a few weekends of exploring the Essex hinterland, we all agreed on a plot on the London side of the village of Chigwell. The village truly was the end of London at that time – at the far end of it, the London speed limit came to an end, and the farmland began. It was a ritzy little enclave with some elegant eighteenth and nineteenth century country mansions, and some very large newer houses where the nouveau riche of East London were moving in.

With great foresight, in the 1930's London Transport had decided to extend the Central Line of the London Underground to the far outer reaches of the city, and there was a station in Chigwell. You could hop on the tube and be in the center of London in fifty minutes.

I was surprised how much my mother liked Chigwell, where there were few Jews, and the atmosphere was semi-rural; it was a world apart from Hightown. But within a week, she was proudly impressing her friends with the news that we were building a new house – in Chigwell.

Building a house? All of my parents' friends were surprised to hear that. This was a very unusual thing to do in Britain, and it's still so rare that my father remains the only person I have ever known who built a new house. It was something else very American about him.

He and my mother very quickly selected a contractor, the contractor knew an architect, and the

House Adventure began in earnest. My parents liked my ideas for the house, and to my surprise, so did the architect.

This was the point at which my mother stepped in. She had always handled the family finances, negotiating car and real estate loans, and now she set up the construction loan so that it automatically became a mortgage on completion of the building work. My father had little interest in or aptitude for finance and he trusted my mother completely.

In their relationship, it was normal for my mother to share the responsibility in the most serious family matters and consequently, to me that role always seemed normal for a woman in a relationship. But it wasn't only the big issues that they shared; in my family home, in pronounced contrast to my friends' homes, my mother did the cooking, but my father washed the dishes. In later life, in my own relationships, that was way that things were organized.

*

Our architect produced some elevation sketches of the new house, and simple drawings to show the layout of the rooms. After a few meetings to agree changes to the design, the plans were finalized, and a meeting was arranged to close the deal with the contractor. My father didn't even bother to go to that meeting, and I went with my mother instead of him. I almost felt sorry for the contractor as she bargained with him; he didn't realize that he was up against decades of the Cohen family's inherited negotiating skills. By the time we left, I wondered if he was going to make any money out of the project at all!

The building permit was quickly obtained, and construction began. Every Sunday morning, we drove to Chigwell, to inspect progress. At first, when the foundation was laid out, and the water, heating and utility lines were set out, my mother took one look, then sat in the car and read a magazine. But as the weeks went by and the brick building took shape, even she became excited. One Sunday, she walked into the space that was to be the kitchen, and stared out into the expanse of mud that was to be the garden.

I watched her, she smiled slowly, for the first time her new house had become a reality. Then she turned and moved into another space. 'This is the dining room, isn't it,' she said, working it out for the first time.

I moved ahead of her, into a larger space, 'Yes, and this is the living room,' I said.

She nodded and smiled again, this time at me, 'It's going to be marvelous, isn't it, Francis.'

'It is,' I said. 'Marvelous!'

The life my father had led her into had turned into the very adventure she had imagined when she first met him. From then on her interest in the house was as great as mine and my father's.

*

26 My Career Begins

Now that I was sold on a career as a lawyer, the next question was, where I was going to study. I was then seventeen and my social life had moved way beyond the Winter and Harmonic Halls in East Ham. I was now used to hanging out in the prestigious areas of Kensington and Hampstead where my friends' families lived, I had discovered sex and jazz, and I was spending every Friday and Saturday evening in London jazz clubs. I loved those sweaty basements and the girls I met there, and the prospect of leaving all that excitement for three years for what I thought of as 'some provincial little town sixty miles from London' – i.e., Oxford or Cambridge – appalled me.

Never mind academic prestige, never mind that my friends were all excited about going to Oxford or Cambridge, I didn't want to leave London, and I finally told my father and mother that I was determined to go to the London School of Economics. To my surprise, they agreed.

I entered the London School of Economics with high hopes, pleased that I got into the college of my choice, full of anticipation about a new stage in my life.

Perhaps my hopes were too high. I wanted to like LSE, but slowly I had to admit that I didn't like it at all. I didn't much care for my fellow-students, I had become a smart Londoner, and they were almost all from the provinces and I found them very naïve. In one of my lectures, I sat next to a quiet young man from Wales and later had lunch with him in the commissary. 'So how do you like being in London?' I asked him.

'I'm from the Valleys,' he said, meaning the small mining towns of Wales. 'All this is very strange to me,' he continued. I almost rolled my eyes!

I was one of the few students who had a car, or who had ever been to another country. This was 1953, remember. I did make two interesting friends, a clever and bluff Yorkshireman, Chris Mercer, who played jazz trumpet and spoke longingly of Tetleys, the famous Yorkshire beer.

'Can't get a good glass of ale in London,' Chris would complain.

I was born in the next county, Lancashire, so I would ritually retort, 'The only good thing that's ever come out of Yorkshire is the road to Lancashire!' And we'd laugh.

My other friend was quite different. Irving Teitelbaum was Jewish, from a town just outside London, and his parents, Lydia and Lionel, owned a dress store, called naturally, ElanEl. Irving was a natural sophisticate, well read, irresistibly charming and warm-hearted. He was the only one of the three of us destined to practice law.

Gradually, as I went to lectures, wrote essays and talked to my tutor, I began to accept that a legal career was not going to be for me. The prospect of being a lawyer for the next forty years positively intimidated me. I was still enjoying London life, the jazz clubs, girl friends, above all spending more and more time at the National Film Theatre, and gradually becoming more certain that I was going to spend my life making films.

At LSE, the year dragged past at a snail's pace and I

became increasingly depressed as I wondered how I was going to tell my parents that I wanted to drop out. Would they understand? In their different ways, my university career meant so much to them. I was then the only Cohen descendant who had been to a university, and my father could not imagine a life without a university education.

As the end of the first year approached, the Intermediate Law examination loomed. It was not possible to switch to another subject, and if you failed the exam, you were out; there were no second chances in Britain. After some thought, that fact became the solution to my problem. I stopped studying for the exam, didn't even take it, and a few weeks later when the results were out, I steeled myself to give my parents the shocking lie: I had failed and that was the end of my LSE career.

My mother was simply stunned. She had been mentally rehearsing a 'my-son-the-lawyer' speech for a year – and now had to accept that I would not be the first university-educated Cohen. My father was simply baffled: he just could not believe that his extremely intelligent and capable son could have failed a first year law exam.

But their attitude surprised me: I had expected anger from my father, perhaps tearful disappointment from my mother, instead what I got was support. 'Whatever you want to do, son, we'll help you in any way we can,' said my father.

More pointedly, my mother asked, 'What *do* you want to do?'

I felt that if ever there was a moment to come clean, this was it. 'I want to make films,' I said.

There was a silence and I felt that this was the answer they had been expecting, perhaps dreading.

'I don't know how you do that,' said my father. My mother said, 'We don't know anybody in films.'

This was before there were any film schools, so there was no academic solution to this problem, no clear career path. In a strange role reversal, I tried to reassure them.

'I'll figure it out,' I said. 'Lots of people *do* work on films, so it must be possible.'

One of the most valuable things I had learned from my father, watching the way he set up the move to Chigwell, was that you had to plan your life and not just let it happen. I did have a plan, but I wasn't going to say exactly what it was until I had put the first stage of it into practice.

*

I was nineteen, and the way I spent the next year and a half must have driven my parents crazy, but they rarely showed it. I wrote stories for movies and sent them to film studios – naturally, nothing came of that! I tried everything I could to get into film production, and had a dozen low-paid jobs around the fringes of the industry, which only led to more low-paid jobs. Finally I got a job as a gofer on a children's movie being shot in Ireland, but in the second week, I borrowed the director's car and crashed it – no surprise when I was fired.

But I'd learned enough in that year and a half about what could and could not be done to fine-tune my career plan. I was then twenty, and without admitting it, I had begun to share my parents' apprehension that I would never be able to make a decent living. My plan had to encompass not only my movie ambitions, but also earning enough money to live as least as well as my parents.

Since a head-on approach to the movie business had failed, I decided to take a more oblique swing at it. My first objective was to get a job in advertising. It was 1956 and commercial television had come to Britain – commercial television meant commercials, and they were short films, weren't they?

So my easy first step was obvious: get into advertising. That didn't turn out to be quite as easy as I had imagined. After a few carelessly planned interviews, which went disastrously, I understood that I had to be more serious and more methodical. I spent the next few weeks studying hard in the local library, reading a year's back issues of the two advertising industry magazines and all the books on advertising that I could find. When I returned to my job-seeking efforts, I had a thorough knowledge of the issues advertising people were currently talking and thinking about, and I managed to get interviews with two of the most powerful companies, Lintas and J Walter Thomson.

The fact that I was able to get interviews at all is an interesting comment on that era; a decade later any candidate without a degree would not even have received a response to letters or phone calls. But my research more than made up for my lack of a degree; at my interviews, I was able to surprise the executives I met with my knowledge of their industry. Both companies offered me a job. The opening at JWT was in four months, the one at Lintas was in three weeks. I took Lintas.

I was still living at home, and I had managed to avoid telling my parents about the failure of my previous efforts, so when I announced dramatically, over dinner that night, that I would be moving out of their house in three weeks because I had an actual job, a traineeship no less, and a future in a real industry that they could understand – well 'overjoyed' doesn't come close to their reaction. For the first time, I knew that I was on my way in life – and they knew it too.

*

27 Meeting Racism, London 1958

At around 1 a.m. one morning in 1958, I had been out for the evening in London's West End with a couple of friends. We were driving down Shaftesbury Avenue in the theater district, when we passed three very attractive, well dressed young black women standing at a bus stop. My friend Charlie Gale, who was driving, saw them, and immediately stopped and backed the car up.

I opened my window, leaned out, smiled cheerfully and told them, 'You're wasting your time at that bus stop, ladies, there'll be no more buses tonight!'

At first they tried to ignore us, pointedly staring over the top of the car as if we weren't there, until one of them gave up and said in a New York accent, 'There's really no more buses?'

I explained that the last bus had gone about an hour ago, and after a few minutes of conversation, we convinced them that we weren't potential rapists or homicidal maniacs, and they agreed to accept a ride back to their hotel near Victoria Station.

They were dancers, on tour with what we'd now think was the archaically-named New York Negro Ballet. They were a little older than we were, very lively and sexy and exotic, and we were pretty excited by them. We arranged to meet them another evening and decided to show them a traditional, good quality English pub. We took them to the famous Red Lion in the fashionable Mayfair district. In those days, the Red Lion wasn't a tourist hangout and most of the customers were well off, upper-class, people who lived locally. In our naivete, we hadn't given a second's thought to what kind of reception we might get there.

The instant we walked in and the other customers saw three black women, their conversation began to die out. As the silence rolled eerily in front of us like a movie special effect, I began to feel a strange combination of uneasiness and anger. I walked up to the bar to order some drinks, but before I could speak, the bartender, I'll never forget his slick, clammy smile, said, 'I'm sorry, I can't serve you, sir.'

I was stunned and enraged, and asked him why not. He just repeated, with his awful fixed grin, 'I'm sorry, I can't serve you, sir.' I knew enough about the law to know that it was illegal to refuse to serve anyone in Britain, and trying to keep my voice calm, I said, 'You *can* serve us, and you will!'

There was an immediate chorus of well-bred English voices shouting, 'Don't serve em, Freddie!' and 'Chuck em out!'

I stepped forward, about to explode, when one of the girls, Georgia, grabbed my arm and said quietly, 'Please don't start any trouble. I wouldn't drink in here if I was dying of thirst!' We reluctantly turned and filed out, feeling humiliated and defeated, with the jolly English patrons shouting, 'Yeah, that was telling em!' 'Cheeky sods!'

Out in the street, we found ourselves in two groups. My friends and I were shaking with anger at our helplessness, and at our guilt in taking the women into that situation. Charlie said, 'We're going to come back here tomorrow night without you ladies, and sort this out!' But for the dancers this was a commonplace of their lives, their faces were imprinted only with resignation, and ironically they were the ones trying to calm *us* down. We reluctantly got back into our cars and drove to an Indian restaurant, where we guessed we be safe from further slights. I'm still ashamed that we never did go back to the Red Lion and 'sort it out'.

With the empty arrogance of twenty-two year olds, my friends and I thought that we were sophisticated, well-traveled men of the world. Now we realized what sheltered lives we had led. The immigrant stream from the Caribbean had not yet reached its full flood, and black people were still a comparative rarity in London, and our only direct experience of them was when we occasionally talked to musicians in the jazz clubs we regularly went to. For us, those black men were the epitome of cool, leading exciting bohemian lives. They were the only people we ever encountered in that pre-Pill and pre-Rock era who were at ease in the forbidden worlds of drugs and casual sex.

We were proud of that sliver of acquaintance across the racial divide, but we had no accurate picture of the lives of black people in the US; worse, we had some kind of fantasy that as artists, the black people we had heard about and admired so much, like Miles Davis or Dizzy Gillespie, were entirely unaffected by racism.

Over dinner, the dancers disabused us of our illusions, and told us stories of the many humiliations they had been subjected to. The most recent was that their ballet company in New York had sent all their toe-shoe measurements to London so that the dance shoe store there could have new shoes ready for them when they arrived; but the British company had refused to believe that blacks could dance on point – and so didn't bother to make any shoes for them.

I became angry again, but Georgia told me, 'You'll get over it. We're used to it, happens all the time.'

I thought this was a terrible thing to get used to and somehow it made me feel much closer to her, which wasn't difficult because she was a very beautiful and elegant young woman. The following night, in a gesture of solidarity, I invited her to dinner at my parents' home.

I picked Georgia up at her hotel and we drove out to Chigwell, but when we got to the house, I found that I had forgotten my front door key. I rang the doorbell and my mother, who knew that I was bringing a friend for dinner, opened the door, already smiling.

But when she saw Georgia, that smile froze. She swayed ever so slightly. I thought she was going to faint, and I realized that when I told her about my date, I had not mentioned that she was black. Instinctively I stretched my arm out to grab my mother if I had to, but almost instantly she recovered herself, regained her broad smile and said, 'Come on in, dear! What's your name? I'm Sally!'

Her shock had lasted only a fraction of a second, but I felt sure that Georgia had seen it, and that the evening had got off to a ghastly start.

Not so. When I introduced Georgia to my father, he looked pleased to meet this beautiful and elegant young woman, and he was his usual courteous, charming self, without a moment of hesitation, a very different reaction from my mother's. At the time, I thought the difference between them was evidence of his greater education and wider horizons.

We had a very pleasant dinner, talking about Georgia's dance company and the weather in England and music and nothing much else that I can remember.

But now, when I look back on that evening, I see it very differently. My father offered no comments on his life in New York, and asked my date nothing about the city where he had studied, lived with his family, and opened his first doctor's office. As surprising as that is, so is the fact that I didn't mention New York myself; I knew my father had been to NY. It would have been so natural to ask him if he knew the New York neighborhood where she lived, or to get them talking about the changes in the city since he had lived there himself. Was I so self-involved, or so smitten with Georgia, that I had no curiosity about my father's past?

Neither my father nor my mother ever said anything to me later about Georgia's race. I saw her for a few more evenings and then she left for Europe with the ballet company to start their tour. We promised to keep in touch, but we didn't. I suppose that my parents knew that was the way it would go.

Now I know the truth of my father's life, I think that when he met Georgia that evening, in spite of his smooth, unruffled demeanor, he must have been infinitely more shocked than my mother. After all the trouble he had taken to slip through the racial net into white society, the humiliations, the three medical schools, the move to another country, all the lying about his entire life before we knew him, after all that, here was his white, liberal son-and-heir waltzing into the family home with a black princess! For all he knew, any moment now I might be throwing the black genes right back into the mix again.

But none of those turbulent, dismaying thoughts could be read from his charming treatment of Georgia or from the attention he paid to her over dinner. At this distance I'm lost in admiration for his immense cool, but what I didn't know was that he had already had a lifetime of practice in the art of concealing his feelings.

As for Georgia, she became a celebrated dancer with the Alvin Ailey Company, and was the first black dancer in the New York City Ballet. I really should have kept in touch with her.

*

Now I had my job, my first 'real' job, I had decided to move out of Chigwell, but it was a while before I found somewhere to live near my office. I found myself a cheap bed-sitting room in Marble Arch, a five minute walk from Lintas, and a five minute walk to the Central Line, and an hour on the tube direct to Chigwell.

Lintas had a formal training program and I moved from department to department, spending a couple of weeks in each, learning the business before landing where I wanted, in a copy group. I began to write radio commercials, and felt that I was closing on the next phase of my plan.

My parents had settled into their new home and I quickly settled in at Lintas. Quietly, my father loved his new house, my mother had grown to love it too, they were both proud of it, proud of their status among their friends.

My father loved his work, he loved his wife and son, and we loved him. We were not wealthy, but my parents were never short of money, and felt completely secure financially. They had fun, driving into London for dinner and the theater, and taking weekends trips to seaside towns.

My father loved to park overlooking the ocean, where they would both sit and read for hours, their usual mix of romance novels and tabloid newspapers for my mother, medical journals, thrillers and Western novels for my father. Every so often, he would break off from his reading to gaze out at the sea, recalling I'm sure, the Caribbean boyhood he never spoke of.

*

I did well in advertising, I liked the work and didn't find it difficult. My colleagues were clever and amusing, and I learned something new every day. But the fact remained, I still wanted to make films.

In the course of my work as the writer and sometimes the producer of commercials, I made friends with some of the younger, professional technicians.

And I started to save money to make my own film. In the twenty-first century, it's commonplace for people of all ages and backgrounds to make their own films – in the early 60's, that was unheard of. I was still seeing every film I could, and deeply impressed with the movies of the French Nouvelle Vague directors: Claude Chabrol's 1958 *Le Beau Serge*,

Francois Truffaut's *The Four Hundred Blows*, and particularly Jean-Luc Godard's *Breathless*. Later in my own career, I was lucky enough to make a documentary film with and about Godard, and later still I worked with the famous French production manager, Serge LeBeau, the inspiration for the Chabrol film.

I made a couple of five-minute shorts as a sort of rehearsal, and then I started to shoot my magnum opus, a thirty minute film. On January 13th, 1961, I shot the first shot in my Marble Arch basement flat, with the lead being played by my friend Charlie Gale, and the second lead by my friend Bernie Cooper, who was to become my lifelong writing partner.

So I had started, but thereafter progress faltered a little.

I spent some of my film savings on a new car and on a long holiday in the South of France. The advertising life was fun, I had an expense account, I enjoyed the work and found it easy – I lost my focus on the film. Also, I had decided to shoot the film on 35mm – like a 'real' movie! – which was beginning to feel like a mistake. The film stock and processing were very expensive, and so was equipment rental. Most documentaries and short films of the period were shot on 16mm, which was much cheaper, with more compact equipment that was easier to handle. But my thinking was that the finished film would be taken more seriously if it was on 35mm.

I couldn't afford to pay anyone, just the cost of the stock and equipment hire was cleaning me out. I also made mistakes that had to be re-shot. I had become my own film school, learning slowly and expensively as I blundered along. At one point, I had a major re-think on the script and had to start all over again.

The net result was that when I went to the South of France for my holiday the next year, 1962, I was deeply embarrassed when I encountered people on the beach whom I'd met the year before. They remembered that I had been making a film last summer and enthusiastically asked how it had turned out. I made some feeble excuses about running out of money, actors' illnesses, and so on. I should be thankful to them: I still remember their skeptical looks, and those looks provoked my determination that when I got back to London I'd throw myself into finishing the film. If they were there in 1963, I was determined that I'd bring a copy of the film for them.

Back home, I was working hard at the agency, where I had been promoted to a commercials producer, and I was going out most nights and pursuing more than one interesting young woman. Typically, by the time the weekend came, I was exhausted – and weekends were when I had to shoot scenes for my film. My father was a lifelong early riser, and I had to enlist his help to make sure that that I got up in time to drive into London and meet my unpaid actors and crew. His job was to bang on my door on Saturday and Sunday mornings and get me out of the house.

I'll never forget those knocks on my door, and I still hear his voice, with his North American accent, and just the slightest Caribbean rhythm: 'Time's gone, sonny Jim! You better get up if you want to make that film!'

He knew nothing about the film business and he was perfectly happy with the progress I was making in my advertising career, but he knew that 'the film' was important to me. I had impressed him with my ambition and the way I was looking to my future – and he was going to do everything he could to help me get 'the film' made.

When I heard his knock on my door, I would groan, and haul myself out of bed, stagger into the bathroom, and by the time I got downstairs he'd made my breakfast. He didn't ask how the film was going or what I was shooting. It was a long while before I understood that not asking questions was his way of showing his confidence in me.

*

28 My Father's Death

My father went to work one day and never came back.

In February 1962, he was driving a 1961 Air Force Blue Mini, which I had persuaded him was the latest in car technology. Its size was ideal for his work, for making those house calls in East Ham's narrow streets, where he often had to make three-point turns, and although it had little power, it handled well enough for him to have a little fun on his seven mile commute between Chigwell and his office in East Ham.

In persuading him to buy the car, I had given little thought to how safe it might be. In that naive era, before air-bags and seat belts and ABS, all cars were assumed to be either as safe or as unsafe as each other.

But my father was then was seventy-seven years old, and he could no longer turn his head as easily or far as he used to; I now have exactly the same trouble myself. In his case, this relatively small disability proved to be fatal.

One Friday morning in winter, when he had driven half of the seven mile commute to his office in East Ham, he came to a wide, busy road in the suburb of Wanstead, which he had to cross. He stopped at the intersection, looked around, but he didn't turn his head far enough to his right to see an approaching motor cycle. It hit the Mini square in the middle of the driver's door. The rider somersaulted over the top of the car and miraculously landed on his feet to watch the rest of the accident.

The motorcycle crushed the driver's door, so flimsy in those pre-door-bar days, and broke my father's right leg, jamming it on the accelerator. The Mini shot forward across the road, out of control and crashed hard into a garden wall. My father wore no seatbelt and his chest was crushed against the steering wheel.

I was called out of a meeting at the advertising agency to answer an 'urgent phone call'. It was my mother. I immediately had a premonition of what she was going to say.

A few days before, home for the weekend in Chigwell, I woke to find that it had snowed during the night. Over breakfast on Monday morning, I offered to drive my father to work; it was a routine we often had in bad weather. I would be his chauffeur, driving him in his Mini to his office, where I would leave him with the car. Then I'd walk to the East Ham tube station, take the tube to work, and in the evening I'd take a different tube line back to Chigwell, where I'd pick up my own car.

But on this particular day, the temperature dropped, and although my father was fit and strong for his age, I didn't like the idea of him driving himself home on snowy roads in the dark. Beyond the London suburbs, there was much less traffic than in the crowded central areas, it was semi-rural with fewer buildings and the fallen snow had a tendency to hang around longer and freeze sooner. In the late afternoon, I called and asked if he'd like me to return via East Ham, and drive him back to Chigwell. I still can hear the pleasure in his voice as he said, 'Yes, Please!'

So that was what I did. We spent a pleasant family evening in Chigwell, and at the end of the evening, when there was virtually no traffic, I drove back into the centre of London on roads that were still slippery, but deserted.

But now, a few days later, this phone call; my father had been involved in a car accident. 'Is it serious?' I asked my mother. 'It's not good,' she said, 'not good at all, Francis.'

I ran out of the my office and drove out through icy streets to the hospital in suburban Brentwood, Essex. It was a cold, gray day and I was in a somber mood. In a drab hospital room, my mother sat nervously beside my father's bed. His body was outlined under the sheet and I could see from the angle of his right leg that it had not yet been re-set.

The doctor told me that he had broken his ribs as well as his leg, but that he was fit and should make a full recovery. He was breathing with difficulty, and his eyes were closed, but he opened them when he heard my voice. He said he wasn't in pain, and then, 'I guess I must have made a mess of the car.'

'Don't worry about the damn car!' I told him. 'Just get well and let's get you out of here.'

His eyes slowly closed again as he drifted off to sleep. I had no idea that those few words were to be the last we ever exchanged.

After a gloomy dinner back in Chigwell, my mother and I both decided to get an early night. I was woken at 7 a.m. by my mother shaking me and crying, 'You've lost the best friend you ever had!' One of my father's broken ribs had pierced his lung during the night and he had died.

I didn't cry, I was too busy trying to calm my mother. My head was aching, not simply with trying to comprehend the loss of my father, but also because I knew that my life had abruptly changed irrevocably and I was deeply apprehensive at the thought of being left alone with my mother.

We had never been friends, and I had always believed it was because I was so much more like my father. Over the next couple of years as I struggled to make an accommodation with her – the compromises were inevitably going to be on my side – I slowly understood that the real problem was that I was actually so much like *her*.

But now that we were thrown together, by my sense of obligation to her as much as by anything else, I was forced to admit to myself how little I knew of her: slowly I became fascinated by, and came to appreciate her many remarkable qualities.

In a sense, my father's obvious attractions had obscured her. Since his absence from my life during the Second World War, although I saw him as much as possible in the following years, I always felt that we never had enough time together. Now there would be no more time together, and all those conversations that I had imagined in some foggy corner of my mind, that we would have one day, exploring all those areas of life, and especially his life, which we had never discussed, would now never take place.

But at the time of his death I had no idea of the immense significance of that loss, or that some forty years later I would still be trying to puzzle him out.

*

Later that year, I finally finished shooting my short film, which I called *Just One More Time*. When I cut it together it ran for more than thirty minutes. I showed it to my friend Fred Burnley, then a trainee editor, and he told me that it was too long and suggested some cuts.

I made the cuts and a few days later showed the film to him again. 'Still too long!' he said. 'You're too in love with it to be as ruthless as you need to be. Let me do it.'

I hesitated, but I knew he was right. 'Don't be *too* ruthless!' I pleaded. He smiled, picked up the film cans and left. Two weeks later we met again and I asked how much he had cut out.

'Don't get hung up on numbers,' he said. 'Just see if you like it.'

I did like it, it didn't seem much shorter but it moved much faster; now, it was the film I'd seen in my head before I started. It was mostly shot in the streets, with a hand-held camera and a lot of it was jump-cut, very Jean-Luc Godard.

'Great job, Fred!' I said. 'Huge improvement, how much did you take out?'

'Five minutes,' he said.

'*Five minutes*!'

'You like it, don't you?'

'Yes. Yes, I do.'

He shrugged and smiled; I smiled too. The remaining twenty-five minutes was to change my life.

That summer, I took a copy of the film to the beach at La Garoupe, at Cap d'Antibes, and proudly gave it to my French summer friends. I gained their respect and recovered my own for myself.

The film was screened at the London Film Festival, a short extract was used on a network tv show about short films, and I got a deal for it to be shown with the London run of Francois Truffaut's *Jules et Jim*. My mother went to see it both at the Festival and in the movie theater. Both times the audience applauded loudly and when the lights went up, she smiled excitedly at me, and said, 'You did it, Francis, you really did it!'

I couldn't help admiring the way she made life work for her; she had totally set aside her disappointment that I had not become a lawyer, and I could already hear her talking about My Son The Film Director...

Just One More Time got applause at every screening, but all I heard was my father knocking on my bedroom door, saying, 'Time's gone, Sonny Jim!' If only he could have heard that applause.

After the London opening, the film got a great review in the *Observer* newspaper and I got a call from a television network for an interview. They offered me a contract to make documentary films and after some haggling over the money we closed a deal. When I told the advertising agency where I was then working that I was leaving, they offered to promote me to Head of Television. I was flattered, I was very tempted, but I didn't change my mind.

I was twenty-six and I was the first freelance documentary director in British television.

*

29 The Hug – In Kalamazoo

By 2010, I had a great deal of new information about my father, but it was like a mosaic, with some of the tiles missing: he was still out of focus, familiar yet strangely enigmatic. My researches had revealed that he was born not in Canada, but like his parents and grandmother, in Barbados; and that he was partly of African slave descent. But because we had never talked about his earlier life before he came to Britain, I had no idea of his feelings about it.

I wondered if he had ever thought of telling me about his real past, if he ever worried that some incident might trigger questions that were impossible to evade. There must have been many times when he considered telling me his real life story. Or perhaps he never thought about it at all, and was simply resolute in his deception. I just didn't know.

If only I could talk to people who knew him! But everyone who knew anything about his past, especially before he came to Britain, was long dead. I wondered if any surviving descendant from his side of the family could throw some light on some of the mysteries. If I could find them...

Uncle Norman, my father's half-brother, had died in Trinidad in the 1960's, and his son, Robert Brewster, had died childless in Trinidad in the 1980's. My Uncle Evan's son, my other cousin Robert – both my cousins were named for our great-grandfather – also died around 1980. I knew that he had children, daughters, but I had no idea how many they were or where they were; and of course if they had married, they would have different surnames.

I searched endless phone listings, looking for anyone called Megahy. Eventually, I found a listing for a Betty Megahy, living outside San Diego. A faint recollection came back to me, of a phone call from my mother during one of my early visits to Los Angeles, in 1979. At the time, there was a television strike in Britain and I was in Los Angeles, trying to find some movie work.

My mother's call was to tell me that Cousin Robert was living in San Diego, and that this couldn't be far from Los Angeles and why didn't I arrange to meet him? I knew almost nothing about Cousin Robert, and what little I did know gave me no encouragement to interrupt my search for work to look him up – and I didn't.

Now, I found myself thinking that if only I had taken the trouble to make that two-hour drive south to San Diego in 1979, my conversation with Robert could have turned to the family background, and I might have discovered the truth about my father there and then. Or would Robert have perpetuated my father's lies?

I was sure that during his time at Harrow, when he spent his vacations with my father and the Cohen family, that he had not let slip details of the Megahys' origins in Barbados. But in 1979, both his father and mine were dead, and we were both grown men – would he have revealed the truth? Well, I didn't take that drive, so I'll never know. But the incident did shed light light on one uncertainty: whether or not my mother Knew. If she truly had known, why would she have suggested a meeting with Robert, with its attendant risk that I could have finally discovered the truth? I became convinced that she didn't know.

Now, in 2010, here was this 'Betty' in San Diego.

I called her, and from her voice I could tell that she was an older person. I told her who I was, and that I had a cousin called Robert Megahy and asked if she knew anything about the family. 'I was his last wife,' she said quietly.

I grew excited and fired off a lot of questions. 'But I know hardly anything about the family!' she told me. 'I only married him at the end of his life.'

'Did you know his father?'

No, she didn't and she seemed reluctant to talk about Robert. I asked her if she had any family photographs that he might have left. No, she didn't. 'Then how about his daughters?'

'There are three of them and they're in Kalamazoo, Michigan,' she told me.

'Great! Do you know how I can get in touch with them?'

No, she didn't. And I was right, they were all married, but no, she didn't have any idea of the names of the men they had married. I put the phone down, thinking that I should go and see Betty at some point, but I doubted I'd find out much about my father from her. No, I had to track down Robert's daughters. I knew that they would lead me back to Uncle Evan, and that somehow by this route I was going to find out more about my father.

I decided to put an advertisement in a local newspaper, *The Kalamazoo Gazette*, for four weeks:

MEGAHY - I'm trying to locate relatives with this name. Write to me at my e-mail address.

Three weeks later, I received this e-mail from a 'D.

Young':

my name is megahy. who are you? where are you from?

And on the same day, I got another e-mail from an SM Scott:

hello, my maiden name is megahy? what an odd thing to see in print, it was in the kalamazoo gazette. I would like to hear from you too. where are you writing from? as far as I know my father only had relatives over seas not in the USA. SJS

I wrote back to both of them, to tell them I was their father's cousin, and got this reply from a woman I came to know as Patti:

francis, my name is patricia megahy. my grandfather was Dr. James Aubrey [Evan] Megahy. He lived in Chicago, Ill. for most of my fathers life. I have photos of a james megahy and a francis megahy's tombstones in the cemetery in barbados. with this much known I'm sure we know others please tell me more about yourself and what you know. anxious to hear all you have to tell. I live in michigan.

And from the woman I came to know as SaraJane:

-YES!!! this is so exciting, I was just looking in some of my father's (Bob Megahy) papers and he saved a letter or card sent from you sometime before he was married to my mother. I knew your name and when my sister called me about the ad I said I wonder if it is my dad's cousin Francis. small world, I have a family tree also written by my grandpa James Evan Megahy in chicago, I will dig it out and try to send it to you. It has names as far back as Barbados and tells where they died. I am the last name on the list as dad had three girls and no siblings.

I was so excited to hear from you. I am SaraJane Megahy, now Scott, and I am married with 2 boys ages 14 and 11. my husband Steve, is 45 and I am 44. when did you start this search and what brought you to california? do you like it out there, we are hoping for snow as we are going skiing in upper michigan this weekend. My sisters are Merry susan Megahy and Patti anne Megahy. you can tell my thoughts are scattered I am rambling on I will try to get that family tree in the mail soon, Sara Scott

Well, I didn't learn a lot from these e-mails, but soon we were exchanging phone calls, and I discovered that all three daughters indeed lived in Kalamazoo, and even more exciting, their mother, Cousin Robert's second wife, Henrymae, the woman with whom he had spent most of his life, was still alive and also lived in Kalamazoo. If Betty Megahy had told me that Robert's previous wife was still alive, I could have simply found her telephone number. But Betty didn't mention her and because Robert was dead, I mistakenly assumed she too must be dead.

Anyway, I called Henrymae and introduced myself, and she seemed to be pleased to hear from me, but I didn't raise the question of race with her or any of her daughters when I later spoke with them. Their warmth and enthusiasm for me, and their desire to meet me, surprised me with its intensity. I knew that I had to go to Kalamazoo to meet them, and when I learned that one of Patti's four daughters was soon to be married, I arranged to go to the wedding.

I flew to Chicago and rented a car for the drive to Kalamazoo. I knew that my father had been to Chicago many times before he made his decision to emigrate to Britain, had been there again in the 1920's, and also on his 1948 Big Trip, and in some irrational way as I drove out of O'Hare airport, I felt closer to him. I was sure that on this visit I was going to make some kind of new discovery about him. I had no idea that I would discover what I could only regard as a family tragedy.

Patti's weekend was completely taken up with her daughter's wedding and so I started out by staying with SaraJane, a very personable, attractive, slightly overweight woman in her early forties, and when I arrived at her suburban house, I had a feeling that I was later to get with all of the Megahy family in Kalamazoo: it was almost as if they were waiting for me to show up some day. Now that I was finally here, SaraJane was clearly thrilled to see me.

She gave me a warm, full-body hug, the kind of hug that a woman only gives to a family member, and it was touching to me to receive this physical welcome from someone who, although she was literally related to me, was nevertheless a complete stranger. This was the typical response I received from my whole family in Kalamazoo. I had nothing in common with any of them culturally or educationally, we were born in and grew up in different countries and had lived wildly different lives; yet they did feel that they were my family, and I felt the same way.

Always skeptical, I had to wonder if this was a counterfeit emotion on my part. Yes, there was a blood link between us, but could I have just thrust myself into any family that I believed was my own and had this same sense of belonging?

There was one undeniable link between Sarajane

and my previous researches. Her father, my cousin Bob, had named her in memory of Sarah Jane, his great-grandmother and mine, who had been freed from slavery as an eleven year old girl. The original Sarah Jane had lived in New York, with her son and daughter-in-law, on West 99th Street, and Robert must have heard a great deal about her, both from his own father and from mine.

SaraJane's young sons were on sleep-overs and her husband was working a late shift at GM, so we spent the early part of that first evening alone together, in her pretty, comfortable house. We talked about my life in Los Angeles, and my work, and her children, gradually closing on the issue hanging in the air between us. We both knew that my visit was really all about race and racism and our family, and I finally worked my way around to The Question: Did you know the family was black?

SaraJane pulled at her hair, thick and a dirty blonde color; then she shook it and it bounced back into tight curls.

'Where else do you think I got this hair?' she asked with a laugh. They all knew that this was going to be a big topic that weekend. If any inhibitions were to be overcome, apparently they were mine.

Henrymae agreed to have dinner with us and we drove over to pick her up, at a small complex of single-story, one-bedroom retirement apartments. She is a straight-backed woman of Cajun descent, almost eighty, with gray hair and a fierce glint in her eye. She opened the door and gave me a broad smile as I told her how excited I was to meet her.

Again, I got The Hug. Then she stepped back

abruptly into her neat living room, and appraised me with a very direct stare.

'You're not a typical Megahy!' she pronounced.

'I'm not?'

She shook her head. 'You're not arrogant like they were.'

I was surprised, 'arrogant' was the last word anyone would have used to describe my father.

'You're a quick judge,' I said.

'It don't take a second to see if somebody's arrogant or not!' Of course, she was judging me by my Uncle Evan and I guessed, by her husband, my cousin Robert.

She gave me another long, hard look. 'We wondered if you were alive or dead,' she said. 'Why did you take this long to find us?'

I grinned, thoroughly charmed by her directness. 'I wasn't looking!' I admitted, and she grinned back at me.

Over dinner, as Henrymae talked about Evan and her dead husband, she told me that Robert had inherited Evan's dictatorial manner.

'He wasn't much of a father,' SaraJane interjected, 'because he didn't have a role model.'

Her sister Merry, the oldest of Robert's three daughters, was later to tell me that 'seeing grandfather [Uncle Evan] was like having an audience with the Pope!'

Henrymae described their regular, ritual Sunday visits to Evan's house. To me, they sounded like joyless occasions, dutiful visits of obligation.

Their lunch always consisted of a roast and mashed potatoes, but as a treat, they would sometimes have peas and rice, special peas that Evan would bring back from his trips to Barbados. Peas and rice! I had a sudden, salivating recollection. My father loved peas and rice, which my mother made for him several times a week. It's a typical West Indian dish, which my mother and I both assumed my father had developed a taste for during his days at Harrison College, not suspecting he had been eating it all his life until he left Barbados for Howard University.

Patti would later tell me that 'we weren't allowed to speak at the lunch table unless he [her grandfather, Uncle Evan] spoke to us first, and after he'd finished eating, he'd just get up and walk out the room without a word.'

But if Evan was harsh with his grandchildren, his wife, my Aunt Mayme, SaraJane's grandmother, made up for it, spoiling them with little gifts and kindness and always a few dollars thrust into each small hand before they left the house.

I was curious about Mayme. 'In her photographs she looks white,' I told them. 'So did Evan, like my father, also marry a white woman?'

Henrymae didn't think so. 'She came from down South,' she said, 'somewhere in Alabama, and I think she was the daughter of a slave and a slave master, because she went to New York to be educated and how could a poor girl like her go to New York to be educated?'

'Did you care what race she was?' I asked quietly.

She shook her head vehemently. 'No way!' she said. 'I'm a Cajun, from Lafayette, Louisiana, and my mother raised me to bear no ill will to any person on account of their race.'

When Mayme got to know her daughter-in-law better, she confided in Henrymae that she was not happy with Evan. 'She said that she never had a marriage after the first seven years,' Henrymae told me, 'but her husband looked after her well, so she stayed with him.'

The implication was clear: Uncle Evan was a womanizer with a number of mistresses, always taking trips to New York and to the 'islands', probably not always on his own, and repeatedly and mysteriously disappearing from the house and reappearing without explanation.

This seemed to be another striking difference between the brothers. I had no reason to doubt that my father had been entirely happy with my mother for the thirty or so years they were together; no reason at all to think that he was a womanizer.

Before we parted that evening, Henrymae told me one new and very surprising fact. 'When I married your cousin,' she said, 'I thought I was his first wife, but I wasn't. He'd been married before. And his first wife was a black girl!'

*

Living the white life: Henrymae (seated left) and her
husband, my cousin Robert Megahy, in the good times

Meeting Henrymae in Kalamazoo

The next day was taken up entirely with the wedding.

Everyone there was white, and I wondered if any of the guests, or the groom, knew of the bride's black ancestry. I met Robert's other daughters, Patti and Merry, and all of their children, but there was no time for talk of the past, this was very much an occasion of the present.

Being at the wedding ceremony and the reception itself was a bizarre experience. I was a complete outsider at this intimate clan celebration, but everyone there on the Megahy side knew who I was. An entire group of people I had never seen before in my life, but they all welcomed me warmly as one of them. During the course of the day and evening I received The Hug many times from Uncle Evan's daughters and grand-daughters.

But immersed in this cheerful and warm group of people, talking to them about their lives, I saw that the upwardly mobile ambitions of the Megahy brothers had not worked out for my uncle's descendants.

Robert had been sent to a prestigious English private school, but there were two differing accounts of what had happened to him after that. I had always heard from my parents that he began to study dentistry, but that his academic career crashed shortly after returning to Chicago, when he informed Uncle Evan that he would not take his dentistry final examinations unless he was given a car.

'If you pass, then I'll give you a car,' Evan told Robert.

'No,' said Robert. 'I want the car now or I won't take the exam!'

'It's your life, son, if you want to throw away your

medical career, that's up to you!'

Father and son were equally obstinate and the result was that Robert never took his finals and never became a dentist. They were victims of their shared genetic intransigence.

In Kalamazoo, I heard a different version of the story; they all believed was that Robert was studying dentistry, realized that it was not for him, and simply dropped out. But the account I had from my parents seemed to fit much better with what I knew of the temperaments of my cousin and my uncle, and I felt that Robert simply gave his family a less embarrassing explanation.

Either way, with his chances of a professional career gone, he became a salesman in the agribusiness, struggling to make a living for the rest of his life, and this seems to have prevented his daughters from having any education beyond high school. They now frankly describe themselves as 'blue collar', although Patti's second husband is an executive with a packaging company. Patti herself works in a Home Depot store, as does her daughter who was getting married to a young man who was also a former Home Depot employee, now trying to find a life as a musician.

I know how disappointed my father was when I 'failed' at my law studies, and how thrilled he was that I later found my own direction in life and was on a upward trajectory when he died.

In contrast, it's easy to imagine Uncle Evan's disappointment at Robert's mundane career. It can only have been made worse when Evan saw me and observed my life in London and realized that whatever academic or other success or failure lay ahead of me, I had at least completely escaped the problems of being black in a white society. I wondered if Evan's feelings had been of envy or resentment, or perhaps even contempt for my father's efforts to pretend that he was something he was not.

On Sunday, I went directly to Henrymae's and during a long conversation with her and Merry, we frankly talked about the Megahy racial heritage. The most startling moment came when Henrymae suddenly announced, 'I don't think even Merry knows this. Now when I met Bob, he was in the US Army in a black regiment. And after he got out of the service and we were married, one day I found him messing with his discharge papers. He was erasing the cross in the 'Colored' box and putting a cross in the 'White' box. I asked him what he was doing, and he turned to me and said, 'I'm trying to get us a better life!''

So my father was not the only Megahy who had 'passed'. I was sure that Robert had been influenced by what he had seen of my father's life during his high school years in England, that the young Harrow schoolboy had learned that it was possible for a light-skinned black man to have a 'better life'.

Henrymae had a number of photographs of Robert, and studying them, I was looking at a man who looked as white as I do, and certainly lived up my mother's opinion of him as good-looking. He had fair hair, almost blond. Yes, it was crinkly, but nobody looking at him would have thought that he anything other than Caucasian.

I found it difficult to believe that he had been in a black regiment, and I wondered if, having married a black woman as his first wife, he later decided, like my father, that he must exploit his light skin to get his family that 'better life'. That decision, to be 'white', could only have further widened the chasm between him and his own father.

Clearly, as children and adolescents, Merry and Patti and Sarajane never gave a thought to what race they were. This was interesting, because their grandfather could easily have made clear, or simply let slip, what was the family's true racial background; he had obviously censored this subject from family conversations.

Before the birth of Robert's daughters, the two men had seen little of each other and Robert harbored a deep resentment of his wealthy father for not helping him to get another career after his refusal to finish his dentistry studies. But when the grandchildren arrived, Evan, and particularly Aunt Mayme, wanted to see those little girls. Robert told his father that the family could be re-united again, provided that their secret was kept. He wanted his daughters to think of themselves as being as white as their skins, and no doubts about it!

Robert's resentment was matched by his father's; Uncle Evan hated to have any restrictions placed on him, particularly by his good-for-nothing son. Both men had only made their agreement to satisfy Aunt Mayme's desire to see her grandchildren. This went a long way to explain the tension of those regular Sunday afternoon visits.

The more I spoke with Henrymae and her daughters, the more it became clear that Robert's life was full of contradictions, and I believe that when they inevitably asserted themselves, they were the main reason that he was never able to fulfill himself.

Patti said that 'he was too clever and well-educated for the life he led.' She described how he would take the children to the library every Saturday morning and spend what seemed like hours looking for books to read during the week. He taught his children to play chess and was interested in the theater and movies. For a while, to make more money, he even ran evening film shows in local movie theaters on his tours of the hinterland. But he spent most of his life working far below his abilities, driving round the baking hot plains of Iowa and Illinois and Michigan, selling fertilizer.

I knew that he must have had ambitions and yearnings beyond both his means and his life. After all, this salesman had been to Harrow school with its echoes of Winston Churchill, where for five formative teenage years he had rubbed shoulders with and felt equal to, the children of London's wealthy, aristocratic and intellectual families.

In a cracked and faded old photograph that my cousin Alma sent me from Israel, there is Robert in the early 1930's, his arm around my Aunt Esther, the perfect Harrow schoolboy, wearing a black jacket and vest and striped trousers, staring confidently at the camera and at a future that must have seemed rich with promise.

He had seen a life so very different from the one he eventually found himself traveling through; he knew only too well what he didn't have. For the first time in his life, in England he had known the freedom of 'passing', of never having to wonder if anyone staring at him could read his true race behind his fair skin and his handsome, clean cut features. The only dark-skinned students at Harrow were the stunningly wealthy Indian princes, royal sons of Maharajahs. It never occurred to his school friends that Robert might be anything but white, but the possibility that someone somehow might work out his true racial identity must always have been on his mind.

When he was drafted into that black regiment in the US Army in 1943, and thus declared officially, undeniably black, he burned with a determination never again to allow anyone's racial definition of him define his life. Just like my father.

After the debacle of Robert's dental studies, Evan seemed to give up on his son; he didn't share his wealth with him in any way that might have changed his life and he didn't help him through his connections with his powerful friends and business acquaintances. But Robert was trying to re-write his life as a white man, and the influential men his father knew were all black, so even if he could have got help from them, he would have once again trapped himself in the black world.

As the pattern of his life settled, it solidified into a long, unrewarding journey from the playing fields of Harrow to the dusty feedlots of the great plains.

The only bright prospect on his grim horizons was the inevitable death of his father, when as the only child, he would inherit everything. Naturally, it didn't work out that way. Robert's mother, Mayme, died in 1966, and three years later Evan became seriously ill and needed twenty-four hour care. Acting out the cliche perfectly, he married his attractive young nurse, and died a few months later, leaving everything to her, other than his debt-encumbered apartment building.

Robert, who had by now divorced Henrymae and married Betty, sold the building and moved to San Francisco with the proceeds, where according to Henrymae he 'lived it up with fine suits in expensive restaurants'. He soon ran through the money, and he and Betty moved to San Diego, where he got a job as a night porter in a hotel. Poignantly, he wrote to his children that he hated San Diego and wished that he had never come to California.

Then he got cancer, and wanted to be near his family, but by now he didn't even have the airfare back to Kalamazoo. His daughters had to send him the money for a ticket and he returned there to die, a forlorn ending to a life that had started with such promise in his London school days. From the descriptions his daughters gave of their relationship with their father, I sensed that among his many disappointments, a major one must have been that he never had any sons; and I'm sure that must have been a great disappointment to Uncle Evan as well.

Robert was virtually an absentee father, 'out of the house every Monday to Friday', said Merry, and he apparently derived little joy from his children. Patti said that 'when we met people, he'd say, 'These are my mutts!' And we felt like mutts.' That was when they were little children and still thought they came from a white family.

As Merry got older, she finally solved the riddle of her ancestry on her own: everything about her grandfather, including his frequent trips to Barbados, now made her think he was of African, and therefore slave descent. She was the first of her siblings to marry and when she became pregnant with her first child, she exclaimed without thinking one day to her younger sisters, 'My God, this child might be black!'

SaraJane and Patti had no idea what she meant, until Merry explained her theories about Evan. With this revelation, so many aspects of their life suddenly made sense to them. Patti told me, 'I don't know why I never thought of this for myself! All grandfather's tenants in his building were black, the people in the streets were black, and the guy in the gas station around the corner from where he lived, where we always stopped to fill up the car on the way home after visiting on Sundays, a man who always had some candies for us kids, he was black too!'

I asked each of them if they were uncomfortable with the idea of their black ancestry. None of them were.

'I figure everybody's sort of mixed up anyway,' said SaraJane. Merry told me that she had recently been to a public meeting where she had proudly stood up and described herself as 'African-American'.

Like me, their discoveries about their racial origins had come after their father's death; like me, nobody looking at them would ever judge them to be black. Acceptance of our true heritage is so much easier for us than for those whose skin tells an indelible story; the decision to acknowledge the truth about ourselves is our own, not society's.

And their ancestry clearly had no awkward or embarrassing meaning for the next generation, Evan's great-grandchildren. SaraJane's younger son had just completed a school project on the family, featuring its slave ancestry. Monica, one of Patti's daughters, had recently taken a Caribbean cruise, and when the ship stopped in Barbados, she eagerly went to look for her great-grandparents' graves.

They were all anxious to know any details that I had discovered, and they were fascinated when I told them that I knew for sure that Evan's grandmother – my great grandmother – was definitely the child of slaves on the Fisher Pond Plantation. They wished me well with my further researches.

Some weeks after I returned to Los Angeles, Merry told me that my visit had provoked a new interest in their family history. All three sisters had decided that they would like to visit their grandfather's grave.

They drove to the cemetery in Chicago and stopped at the gate to ask where his grave was located.

'It's our grandfather's grave,' explained Merry to the black security guard. He gave them a strange look.

'Ladies,' he said, 'I think you in the wrong place!'

*

With Cousin Robert's daughters in Kalamazoo

Sarajane, her husband Steve and the author. She said, "Where do you think I got this hair?"

The Author and Merry, who said, "My God, this child might be black!"

The Author and Patti, who said, "I don't know why I never thought of this for myself!"

30 Standing In My Father's Shoes

On my last day in Kalamazoo, I spent so much time talking with my second cousins SaraJane and Patti that I finally left for the airport much later than I had planned, but I was sure there was still time for an important detour: I was determined to see my Uncle Evan's house.

As I saw Chicago's spectacular skyline angling upwards through the heat haze of a record 86 degree end-of-September day, I was in a reflective, almost melancholy mood. The sincerity and the warmth of the welcome I had received in Kalamazoo was not to be doubted, and my cousin's children and grandchildren all seemed to have found happy lives for themselves there, but in the contrast between Robert's aspirations and his achievements, I saw a tragedy.

Why had he buried himself in Kalamazoo, why didn't he want to succeed and conquer the vibrant, powerful city of his birth? All that pretending about race, all those questions that were never to be asked or answered, all the bottled-up shame, had somehow crippled his ambition, hobbled his will to succeed, muted his energy. He was so handsome, he was smart and educated, he knew a wider world not from his imagination, but from his own experiences, and yet his life had narrowed into itself, had wound down to a penniless, unsatisfied ending in a small town in Michigan. For me, he was just another uncounted victim of racism.

With a heavy heart, I drove on into Chicago itself, the traffic surprisingly speeding up as the road became more crowded. I had no GPS and I was trying to guess which exit I should take for my uncle's house on Michigan Avenue.

I tried to read the street signs, but they came too fast and were often obscured by huge trucks. I was getting hemmed in by other cars and high-sided commercial vehicles, and I began to be overcome by anxiety, anxiety about the time, about the fact that I might not find the house at all, and above all, I was filled with unidentified apprehensions about actually seeing the place, a place where a life had been lived that was so different from mine. I could now see that the tall buildings of The Loop were fast getting closer and I knew that I was too far north.

I suddenly saw a sign for Lake Shore Drive, and because I knew that Michigan Avenue was only one block from it, only one block back from the lake's edge, I swerved across three lanes of angry, honking traffic, towards the lake. But the road I took passed over Michigan Avenue and spat me out onto a maze of highways under construction, littered with confusing detour signs. I tried to turn back, took the first exit I saw and found myself in a massive sports stadium.

Two illegal U-turns later and I found myself at last on Michigan Avenue, but I was on the 2600 block and I was looking for 4533. Michigan is a one-way street and I had my first piece of luck: the one way was the way I needed to go, south. I had no idea why I was driving so fast, I didn't reflect on what apprehensions were preventing me from taking a later plane so that I could make a thorough investigation of the area.

I was almost 20 blocks from the house, but as I raced through the neighborhood I kept trying evaluate it, was it black? It certainly looked it. The traffic slowed and then stopped, ahead of me was the chaos of parents picking up their children from school. I peered through the windshield at the school kids. Yes, they were mostly, but by no means all, black. It had been a black neighborhood when my uncle bought the building sixty years ago, and it was still a black neighborhood.

Gaps opened up and as I raced in and out of the cars again, flooring the accelerator and chirping the rental car's tires at the traffic lights, I wondered why it was so important to me to see the house, and I realized it was because my father had been here.

Suddenly, I was on the 4500 block. In this section, Michigan Avenue is a broad tree-lined street, and on that brilliantly sunny day, with that extra poignancy that comes when you know instinctively that it's the last hot day of the summer, it was easy to imagine it as a two-way street, with very little traffic on it – just as it must have been during most of the time Uncle Evan lived there. It would have been a very pleasant avenue indeed.

I saw a group of young black men hanging out on their stoop, kind of rough-looking, and I peered at their house: was that 4533? No, it was 4525. I drove on a couple of houses farther and there at last was 4533. I stopped the car and got out. However much of a hurry I was in, this was a moment for pause and contemplation.

This was the apartment building I'd heard all the stories about, the building my father stayed at on his 1948 trip, the home to which my cousin Robert and his white wife Henrymae had brought their daughters SaraJane and Mary and Patti for lunch every Sunday, when they were too young to even question their ancestry. I felt a strange excitement – and all I was doing was looking at an apartment building! Oh, but the memories and speculations it conjured up...

I stared at it, a substantial, light-gray stone structure, still looking in pretty good condition. I thought about my father visiting here, easily imagined him walking along this street, and for the first time, I began to wonder what he must have thought of the niche his brother had carved out for himself in Chicago: a black niche.

From what I heard in Kalamazoo, I had formed a good picture of Uncle Evan's life. His work as City Engineer of Chicago brought him into contact with influential local people; from the Funeral Notice that Patti showed me I saw that his mourners and pallbearers were all aldermen and doctors and lawyers. He earned a good living from his City job, from his work as a doctor and from his bank presidency, more than enough to provide for his family and live in a fine style. He was a prominent member of the community – of the black community, that is – a professional man who had a prosperous life, and was fulfilled in his work.

It sounded very much like a life my father might have had if he had remained the US, and it didn't sound so bad. But there was a mystery to Evan's life that I couldn't unravel. His money and his place in Chicago society, it was all dependent on his accepting his blackness, his African heritage, and inevitably that acceptance made him a second-class citizen in his own country. How on earth had this proud, even arrogant man, been prepared to defer to whites whenever they deemed it appropriate?

However prosperous my father might have been in the US, just like Uncle Evan, he would still have been a second-class citizen. At the time of his 1948 visit, an African Colored man – my father's official, US government classification – would have been unable to stay in most hotels in the South, and even as far west as Scottsdale in Arizona. The list of activities forbidden to him in many states was endless – in 1948, he would still not even have been allowed to join the American Medical Association.

Despite all Uncle Evan's money and prestige, in the Chicago of the 1940's a black man, however light-skinned, had no entree into the wider, white society. He could live a comfortable, even affluent life, but it had to be on a parallel track – and those tracks never met. You could be rich, you could have your place in society, but that place was defined by whites – and you'd better know your place, boy!

But unlike my father, superficially at least, Evan appeared to have no problem with his African ancestry. In fact, he was a proud founder of the American West Indian Association. The bank he had founded was in partnership with other black Americans. And yet, and yet... In spite of all that apparent racial pride, at those Sunday lunches attended by Henrymae and Robert and their children, there were forbidden topics of conversation, chief among them Evan's parents and their origins in the Caribbean. What a conundrum my uncle had devised for himself: even as he embraced his ethnicity, he knew that denying it would give his grandchildren a better life.

SaraJane's words came back to me: 'All

grandfather's tenants in his building were black, people in the streets were black, the man at the corner gas station where we stopped to fill up the car every Sunday on our way home, who always had cookies in his pocket for us, he was black too...'

But like me, she had never reflected on any of the seemingly obvious contradictions in her life. Was my friend Susan Weber right? At some early stage in our lives, had SaraJane and I learned that there were questions that would not be answered and that we had better not ask them?

Of course, because I knew nothing of my father's true origins, he and I had never talked about how he felt on his 1948 trip, back in the country of segregation, a country where a black man had to know his place, or he could be in great jeopardy, even his life itself at risk. How did he feel visiting his brother in a black neighborhood, his brother with no pretension to being anything other than black? How did my uncle feel, knowing how different my father's life was? How much did they have in common? I knew from the schools they sent their sons to that they had shared the same intense social aspirations, to metaphorically shed their dark skin.

But you could scarcely have seen a more dramatic contrast in the life they lived than in the family's military service in the Second World War: in the segregated US Army, Evan's son, my cousin Robert was a private in a black regiment; in the British Army, my father was a colonel, and no racial questions asked.

In 1948, when my father visited Chicago, the US Army was still segregated. This was some twelve years before the Civil Rights movement; Martin

Luther King was a still a seminary student. Even more sinister, it was sixteen years before the last recorded lynching in the US.

When my father walked along Michigan Avenue in that hot, humid summer of 1948, after twenty-seven years of living in Britain as a white man, no doubt hearing there so many derogatory references to 'wogs' and yet not being counted as one of them, I can't imagine that there was any sense in which he could have possibly felt at home here in Chicago, with 'his' people.

In England, certainly, nobody would have thought my father was Swedish; but most people would have judged that he might be of Italian or Turkish, or even Egyptian descent. Even the most careful look at him would not have conjured up the word Africa. His perceived race in Britain did not expose him to any kind of discrimination or persecution in his working or social life. But on this Chicago street, in a country and a city so finely attuned to the very minutest varieties of race and skin color, the instant judgement of any passer-by would have been that Ken Megahy was a just a light-skinned black boy.

Was the contrast in the brothers' lives, the one a member of a segregated minority, the other outwardly assimilated into his society, but inwardly uneasy, was this the true source of the tension between them on Evan's visit to London? Was it more important than their obvious temperamental differences? Because for Evan too, the contrast in their lives, in their places in society, must have made a powerful impression.

I was now sure of my analysis of Evan's extraordinarily aggressive and abrasive behavior on his one visit to London, particularly in public: it was because he could get away with it.

By the time Evan made his London visit, five years after my father's visit here, my cousin Robert's career had already failed. Evan was much wealthier than my father, but in London he found the younger brother living the white life with a white wife and a white son. He felt that my father had taken a cowardly decision in rejecting and concealing his racial heritage, and yet in his own way, he had taken a correspondingly cowardly decision himself: very early in his US experiences he had given up contesting the humiliating status that was accorded to a black man in the US.

But he never exposed my father's lies, never told me and my mother that my father was not born in Canada, never mentioned the Fisher Pond Plantation. Once again, he kept his mouth shut, and for damn sure, he resented keeping his brother's secrets.

For such an opinionated and self-satisfied man, after a lifetime of keeping his mouth tightly shut in white company, knowing that he had to, and resenting every single moment of it, his visit to London must have been exhilarating, when just for the hell of it, he could say the most provocative things that came into his head, on buses, on the street, in pubs and museums and banks, simply to see how far he could push the limits.

I looked at Uncle Evan's building a moment longer, then I got my camera from the car and took some shots of the house. I wanted a photograph of myself standing in front of it. I looked back at the young black men on their stoop, and still felt wary about them, and felt guilty about my wariness and my own racism: they were probably just working-class guys home after work and enjoying a beer on a sunny day. For a crazy instant, I had a brief, patronizing fantasy, of walking over to them and saying, 'Hey guys, I'm a brother too, descended from slaves, just like you!' Yeah, sure!

When my father came here in 1948, to 4533 South Michigan Avenue, his feelings were exactly the reverse. He recalled the circumspection, the careful control he had to exercise over his behavior when he was a young man and lived in a segregated society. He re-experienced the restrictions, the stares of assessment from white people, the subjection to their judgment, which had led him to leave the US three decades earlier. After all, it was not until 19 years later, in 1967, that the case of *Loving v Virginia* went all the way to the US Supreme Court and it was established that the states' bans on interracial marriage were unconstitutional. There were 38 of those states, and in those great states of South Carolina and Alabama in 2012 that law is yet to be repealed! The very basis of my father's family life, his marriage, the engine of his aspirations to be one among equals in society, could have sent him to prison for five years.

Standing outside 4533 Michigan Avenue, just as I was now, he felt that the commonplace freedoms he had come to accept as perfectly natural in Britain over the previous decades, had been abruptly revoked in Chicago. Setting foot on US soil, he was once more judged not by the content of his character, but by the color of his skin.

As I stood outside that house sixty years after his visit, it was painful to be dramatically reminded that so many of the issues that had driven my father into his secret life are still unresolved in the US: 25% of black African American men under the age of twenty-five are in prison, on parole, or on probation. Inter-racial suspicions are so hard to eradicate, that I myself had been reluctant to ask the young black men on the stoop to take my photograph.

I had no idea if the two brothers had ever talked about these issues, either in London or in Chicago. I stood outside Evan's house, lost in my thoughts, trying to imagine and understand all the conflicting feelings the two brothers must have felt when they met here. There was love between them, I feel sure, but there was also bitterness on Evan's side.

I still wanted that photograph. I thought I would just have to ask the young black men, but then I saw a hefty, but pretty, young black woman walking toward me, with two small children. I stepped forward, smiled and said, 'Would you mind taking a photograph of me in front of this house?'

I held out the camera. She tilted her head with a suspicious look. Once more the racial barrier had been raised.

'My father used to live here,' I said, encouraging her with a small lie, 'When he was a young man.'

Her face now lit up abruptly with her own smile, and she took the camera from me. I posed, a little self-consciously and she pressed the shutter. 'Could you do another, please?' I asked, 'a little nearer...' She moved closer, pressed the shutter again and then gave the camera back to me.

She took her children's hands and moved on again. I thanked her and started back to the car and then behind me, I heard her say, 'What floor did he live on?'

I spun around, suddenly understanding. She was standing right in front of 4533. '*You* live in the building?' I asked. She nodded. We smiled, a strange, brief connection between us.

'He lived on the first floor,' I said.

Her smile broadened. 'That's my floor!' she said.

'Can I take your picture?' I asked. She hunched slightly with shyness, but posed with her son and daughter. She looked at me and hesitated, then, 'Would you like to see inside?' she asked. I was sorely tempted, but I looked at my watch: I should have been checking in for my flight at this exact moment.

'Thanks, but it'll have to be on my next visit,' I said. 'When will that be?' she asked.

I shrugged, 'I really don't know.'

We smiled and said goodbye, I turned and took another quick shot as the little family walked up the stone steps toward the front door, Uncle Evan's front door. I jumped back into the car, and floored the accelerator, swinging into the traffic, with a sense of achievement, of contentment even, that I couldn't explain. There was a lot to think about on the plane, and if I drove like hell, I might even catch it.

There was a striking parallel between trying to remember every detail of the fleeting impressions I had in front of the house; and trying to project myself into my father's thoughts and feelings when he stood there, in a neighborhood full of black people, outside his black brother's house.

The pressure of having to catch that flight had heightened the experience and compressed it into its vividness and made it so tantalizing for me. However briefly, for a few moments I had truly stood in my father's shoes and seen with his eyes. The feelings I had on that Chicago street brought me closer to understanding him than I had ever been in his lifetime.

*

Uncle Evan's
apartment
building

Michigan Avenue,
Chicago

The author at
Uncle Evan's
building, with
the current
tenants of his
apartment

31 A Mystery Remains

Unraveling so many of my father's secrets had only increased my curiosity about him. I kept wondering what else there might be that I didn't know about him.

In the early stages of my researches I believed, mistakenly, that the central mystery I had to unravel was why a Canadian Doctor with two degrees, would leave his entire North American family behind, and use all his savings to come to Britain, and start all over again in a third medical school?

I thought that there just had to be something specific that drove him to Europe.

Even after I discovered his black African ancestry, even after my visit to Kalamazoo and Chicago, I was sure that this handsome, charming and eligible man, who did not meet my mother until he was forty-five years old, must have had some previous romantic relationships, perhaps even a marriage, and in that case, surely some children?

Exploiting the advantage of my rare surname – there are only two Megahys in the Dublin phone directory and none in London – I began to search the internet for anyone with the same name. Night after night, I scanned different websites and search engines.

And I did find other Megahys. There were some in Canada, but there was nothing to relate him to them. I found a professor Megahy Simpson at USC in Los Angeles, but his family was from Scotland.

There was a Mohammed Megahy in Chicago, but he wrote back to say that his family was from Egypt, and that he had no idea how they had acquired their surname. But sporadically, almost aimlessly, I continued my search. I had no idea what I was looking for, but I knew that I had to keep on looking.

And then one night, on the website for Georgia Tech University, in Atlanta, Georgia, I found an item mentioning a student whose name was Jon Francis Megahy. He had my first name and my surname, could this be merely a coincidence? I wrote to him immediately:

1527 Benedict Canyon
Beverly Hills Ca 90210
I am trying to reach a student at Georgia Tech, John Francis Megahy, who has the same name as I do, to check if we are related.

Can You help?

Several days later, I got this reply:

Good day Mr. Megahy. I apologize for not getting in touch with you sooner. I got the e-mail forward just before Christmas break. I'm not aware of any direct relation, but I'd be more than happy to check. I'm looking forward to your reply. Take care!

Jon F. Megahy

And I wrote back:

Dear Jon F

Thanks for your reply. Ours is a fairly rare name...

I'm trying to trace my father's early life. I know that he went to school at Harrison College in Barbados in the first years of the twentieth century; subsequently became a medical doctor in the US; and he then worked in what was known as the Leeward & Windward Islands, before he emigrated to the UK around 1916.

So I wonder if we have any common ancestors, and what was the origin of your own family and its name...? In my own case, it was from Ireland, but I have found it extremely hard to trace nineteenth century records in Ireland...

I'll be grateful for any information you might have.
Best regards
Francis Megahy

And he replied:

Good Day Mr. Megahy :)

I apologize for the day delay, but I had no new information to provide while my parents sifted through our 'files' and contacted relatives in St. Lucia. My mother's reply is attached below. Please feel free to ask more about anything you want. I'm sure that this is quite an event for both sides of our family.

I've created some online picture resources (photo albums) containing various pictures of my immediate and extended family, other activities, and general info on St. Croix (where I'm from) and St. Lucia (most extended family). Ask me for the URLs if you'd like to see them.

Have A Very Nice Day!

P.s. I'm interested in how you managed to discover my name. I've been searching for Megahys myself and the most I've produced were Megahys in the continental U.S. in the 1700s and 1800s who had emigrated there directly from Ireland.

Jon F. Megahy

From Laureen Megahy:

To: 'jmegahy007@yahoo.com'
Subject: RE: James Kenneth Campbell Megahy
Dear Jon,

Like I said, this is really exciting! The coincidence is too striking!

Even Aunty Monica got goosebumps when we told her, and Daddy almost flipped! You can imagine Aunty Dedette! And we thought we were the only Megahys on this planet!

Aggie said that your great grandfather was a visiting doctor to St. Lucia (a Windward Island) in the early 1900's. He was White, with origins from the UK. He'd come over with other visiting doctors and they'd all stay at the Du'Boulays (a french aristocratic family). Many of those Du'Boulays have since died or returned to France...

Your grandfather (St. George Megahy) was a product of Dr. Megahy's union in 1911 with a St. Lucian woman (Rebecca Joseph) who worked for the Du'Boulays. Your grandfather met his dad only once on a subsequent visit to St. Lucia, then was told he had returned to the UK or somewhere.

We don't know your great grandfather's first name, but we can check your grandfather's (deceased in 1987) birth certificate, if we can find it.

We're hoping the name would be on there...in those days father's name was omitted if the child was illegitimate. Aunty Monica and Aunty Rebecca are doing the research at the St. Lucian registry. Your middle name 'Francis' is for St. Francis of Assisi as well as for your father (Leonard St. George Francis Megahy).

I don't know if this information is useful to Mr. Megahy, but you may want to pass it on.

PS: Congratulations on joining the school band....we're proud of you son!

God Bless

Love

Now I was really getting somewhere, and the mention of St. Lucia brought back the occasion when Marie Claude's sister had visited London and I had introduced her to my father, discovering to my surprise that he spoke fluent French – because he had worked in St Lucia and St Vincent and had to learn French to communicate with his patients. At the time, this all was interesting if not particularly significant, but now that I was in touch with this family from St. Croix, only a hundred and fifty miles from St. Lucia, it seemed very significant.

I knew that my father had worked in St. Lucia – and this Megahy family had a St. Lucia connection. Excited by this new information, I decided to try something obvious that I should have thought of long before: I checked the St. Lucia telephone book to see if there was anyone called Megahy listed there.

Almost immediately, I found a number for a Rebecca Megahy in Castries, the capital. I checked the time zone, to make sure that it wasn't the middle of the night, and with some trepidation, I dialed the number. I waited for an answer, but instead I heard an answering machine.

'Hello, this is Rebecca Megahy,' the voice said. I froze and for the first in my life I knew what the expression 'the hairs on the back of my neck stood up' meant.

I've heard my name mis-pronounced all over the world, not least in the country of my birth. The name is Celtic, Scottish and Irish, and it wasn't until I went to Ireland in the late 1980's to make a movie for MGM, with Pierce Brosnan, that I discovered that like my father and mother, and all of her family, I had always pronounced my own surname incorrectly.

The correct, Irish or Scottish pronunciation is three syllables: Meg-ah-hi, with the first syllable very short, almost M'; and the name can even be spelled McGahy. But my father and mother had always pronounced it in two syllables: Muh-gay... and I had just heard this woman on her answering machine pronouncing it in exactly the same – incorrect – way: Muh-gay: This just couldn't be coincidence!

The next day, my head still full of the implications of that specific mispronunciation, I woke to find an amazing e-mail from John Francis Megahy's mother, Laureen:

Dear Francis,

First let me introduce myself. I'm Jon's mom and the wife of Leonard St. George Francis Megahy, one of St. George's four sons. Our own family tree follows. We have all been very intrigued by this unexpected coincidence. It's exciting to think you could be related to my husband's family. Surely there must be some connection between St. George and your father...the timing, the region and the occupation all make it likely.

We noted your family tree, however we could not corroborate any of the names/events. Just as we feared, St. George's birth/baptismal certificate failed to show his father's name (see below). One thing's for sure, he carried his father's surname all his life and passed it on in marriage.

We found some Megahys on the web from Canada, one of whom is in the Royal Canadian Air Cadets (Tia Megahy). Your tree indicated that some of your ancestors emigrated there. Coincidentally, Jon's passion has always been aviation and that's what had gotten him studying Aeronautical Engineering at Georgia Tech. He'll tell you all about that.

A little about us: Rebecca, Leonard and Monica are all educators. Bernadette's a secretary (me too) at Hess Oil refinery. Melinda is a travel consultant, McArthur is a licensed electrician, Nigel is a professional athlete (cyclist), and not sure what LaRocque does. It may not be a good idea to call Rebecca at Ave Maria School. I suggest you contact her at home (758) 452-4901.

Our only photo of St. George (Leonard's and my wedding - 1980) is enclosed. I attempted to identify all his children in this 21 year old photo. Bernadette (the last) is not identified but she's kneeling immediately in front of Rebecca. The last photo is me.

Warm Regards,

Laureen Megahy

I now had enough information to wonder if it all could be a series of coincidences. Rebecca Joseph had been impregnated in the exact period in which my father was working in St Lucia. She had taken his name, and her descendants all pronounced that name exactly as my father pronounced it. Her child had named his son Francis, after my father's own mother's name. It was too much for me to believe that it was coincidental.

It was perfectly credible that my father would have had a relationship with Rebecca Joseph. His work in St Lucia and St Vincent may have been interesting, but it was a lonely life for a young man of twenty-five; it's not surprising that he sought to amuse himself with the company of the island girls.

But why did he choose as the object, if not of his affections, then at least of his attentions, a poor and unsophisticated girl who earned a living by selling cocoanuts and flowers at his hotel? We must assume that Rebecca Joseph, even if of humble origins, was herself charming and attractive, so was my father simply overcome one night by a young man's irresistible priapic drive?

Even if that was the case, he was after all a doctor, and would have understood – as much in the moment as after it – the likely result of his surrender to his libido. The known facts of his travels merely tell us that he was on the island during the year in which the child was conceived – 1911 – and that the next year, he returned via Barbados to New York, and had no further contact with Rebecca.

Does this mean that he deliberately abandoned his child and the mother?

That would be such a callous act and so unlike the man I knew, but I knew only the mature and mellow man of his middle years. My first recollections of him don't begin until he was in his mid-fifties onwards; and the clearest memories I have of him are all from the period after World War Two when he was in his sixties.

He was a product of his time and environment, a society where 'outside' children, as they still call them in those Caribbean islands, were not at all unusual. The abandonment of a child, which I find so shocking, was and still is, by no means a rare event there, and one that my father's conscience may well have been able to absorb for more easily than I can imagine.

It is perfectly possible that over thirty years earlier,

the easy going man I knew had been a much more driven character, making his way in the world, and already planning to live as a white man. Knowing that a black wife and a child of mixed race would be burdens that could block all his plans, and would definitely prevent him from realizing the dream he already had of a different racial identity, perhaps he had simply decided to sail away from them.

But I never saw the faintest fluctuation or inconsistency in my father's kindness and compassion and since there is no certain information that he knew of the child's existence, my belief is that he did not.

*

32 Meeting Aggie

When Laureen wrote to me to tell me that her mother-in-law, St.George Megahy's widow, Aggie, who is eighty-one, was going to be in Brooklyn for a month, I knew that I had to meet her, so I arranged to stay with my friend Susan Weber in New York at the same time.

As soon as I arrived in Manhattan, I called Aggie. She sounded very lively, but a little circumspect.

'You do know who I am?' I asked her. I knew she was eighty-one, I had no idea of her mental condition, and I was anxious to make sure we didn't start with any misunderstandings.

'Oh, yes! You're my husband's half-brother. You have the same nose!'

So she had that absolutely clear, but I still didn't know how much interest she had in me or in the story generally. We arranged that I would drive out to Flatbush the next morning, and I would take her to lunch.

Susan had very kindly loaned me her chauffeur, Philippe, and a Mercedes station wagon, and I packed a video camera into the back and we drove out across the Brooklyn Bridge, picking our way through the crowded streets on the other side.

As we got to nearer to Flatbush, I saw more and more black faces. Along Flatbush Avenue, there was hardly a white person.

Philippe quickly found the street Aggie was staying on and we parked outside an old brown brick apartment building. I called from the car to say that I was outside and asked which apartment she was in.

'3B', she said. I unloaded the camera and headed for the building. But as I reached the front door, it opened and there was Aggie, smiling, perhaps a little uncertainly. When we spoke the day before, I had told her that I was going to take her to lunch, but it was a little early and anyway, I wanted to shoot an interview with her.

'Aggie,' I said, 'it's great to meet you!' I embraced her, and now I noticed that a very pretty young black teenage girl was standing behind her.

'Who's this?' I asked.

'This is your great-niece, Ashley,' she said.

I embraced Ashley, and she too was a little shy. These women were a little more cautious with their hugs than the women in Kalamazoo had been. Perhaps their confidence in the family connection was lower. I felt cautious myself, as if I had to 'handle' them. Was it, I wondered, because they were black? Was this yet another example of my unconscious racism?

I said, 'It's a little early for lunch. You remember I spoke on the phone about doing an interview with you – can we do that now?'

'Oh, right, that'll be fine,' she said.

Ashley led the way back into the building, which was a little run-down and where the brown theme continued. We took an old creaking elevator to the third floor, and as Ashley dealt with the all the locks on the door, Aggie said, 'Oh, we don't have all this locking business back home. Sometimes we go out and leave the front door not locked at all!'

'That's because we live in a good neighborhood,' said Ashley.

Was she making a point to me? We went inside and

made small talk for a moment, and I was looking at Aggie carefully. I knew that Aggie's name was Mrs. Megahy, but all my life that term had only been used for my mother and this was only the second Mrs. Megahy I had ever met. As a concept, the fact that this old, black woman was probably married to another child of my father's had been easy to handle; the reality of it was somewhat harder to absorb.

But after all, she was my relative by marriage, whereas Ashley was my blood relative: my half-brother's grand-daughter, my father's great-grand-daughter. She was tall, almost my own height, slim and extremely pretty, looking very grown-up for her fourteen years.

For my part, I was trying, and I think succeeding, to be as open and relaxed and friendly as I could, and the two women were quickly at their ease with me.

Inside the apartment, we sat in a dark room, with dark red velvet sofas, and wooden furniture with tinted mirrors. Before we started talking, the phone rang and Ashley answered, almost immediately handing it to me. It was her mother, Laureen. 'I'm here, Laureen,' I said.

'I know, I know!'

I laughed, 'Didn't you think I'd be able to find Flatbush?'

'Well, you know, I wasn't sure!'

After a moment, I hung up and I asked Aggie again if it was definitely going to be all right to record our conversation, and she agreed.

'Are you nervous?' I asked.

'Oh, no,' she said, 'not at all.'

I had a feeling that I was probably transmitting

some uncertainty of my own and that she was simply trying to put *me* at my ease.

We started the interview and Aggie told me that when she met my half-brother, St. George Megahy, his mother Rebecca Joseph, my father's lover, was already dead.

What she knew of my father's 'relationship' with Rebecca, her mother-in-law, came from St George. Rebecca used to deliver coconuts and flowers to the hotel where the visiting doctors, including my father, lived. A relationship developed between her and the young Doctor Megahy, provoking the jealousy of other ladies in Castries. A doctor was a good catch, but then the time came when Doctor Megahy's contract was up, and he left the island.

It was not until after he had left that Rebecca found that she was pregnant. She gave birth to a boy, whom she called St George Francis. All she knew about his father was that he was a doctor and he had left St Lucia for Europe, but she decided to give her baby his father's name, and he became St George Francis Megahy.

St George himself, according to Aggie, was no star. Shortly after she met him, she became pregnant and her family sent her to Brazil, where she remained for 16 years – her child died when he was ten. When she returned to St Lucia, St George seemed to have reformed, he met her at the dock, they married and had four more children. But marriage did not improve my half-brother's behavior, he treated Aggie badly, and was a womanizer. He had no less than four other children with other women – and three of them have the surname Megahy. Aggie had a tough life, and her fortitude and cheerfulness commanded my admiration.

The interview was over, I packed up the camera and we all went down to the car. Now the atmosphere between us was easier.

I told Philippe, 'Let's just cruise and find the best place we can for lunch.' In Flatbush, there's not a lot of choice, but we eventually settled on a Dominican sea-food restaurant.

The most touching moment came with Ashley over that lunch. Mostly, I was speaking with Aggie while Ashley just watched and listened intently. But then, as I ate, she suddenly leaned forward to me and said, 'You're my great-uncle'.

It was a statement, but her tone requested confirmation and I was happy to give it.

'Yes, I certainly am!' I said and we smiled, a complicit smile that had some kind of a family content to it. I think that was the moment when she truly accepted that this old white guy wasn't a stranger, but really was part of her life. It touched me as I had been touched by the hugs of the young women at the wedding in Kalamazoo.

When we exchanged our farewell hugs on the doorstep of the apartment building, Ashley said, 'You have to come to St Croix and meet everybody. You'll have a great time!'

I knew that I would.

There was much to think about on the way home. I wasn't sure that Aggie's comment that I had the same nose as her husband carried much weight, except that it is not a negroid nose. However, I had the feeling that everyone in St Croix *wanted* to believe that we were related.

There were only three possibilities: that somehow St George's mother had arbitrarily taken the 'wrong' name for her child; that there was another doctor with the same name as my father, who mispronounced it in the same way; or that my father was indeed the patriarch of this family. I felt that the pronunciation of the name was the true determining factor, the only convincing scenario.

I called Aggie later in the evening, and Ashley answered the phone. 'Aggie misses you,' she said.

'Then I'd better speak to her.'

Within a moment Aggie said, 'We were talking about you last night and Ashley said she misses you and she wants you to come to St Croix, and I miss you too.'

I was touched that I had had so great an effect on the two women on such a brief meeting, and I began to wonder why. It's too easy to imagine that it's because I am such a charismatic personality. I also had to deal with my own desire to establish this connection.

Was it because I love mysteries and unraveling them? The movies and documentaries I have written and directed have always had that unraveling as a key element. Then, too, there is my own desire for family, was it that?

Neither of those explanations would make any sense for Aggie or Ashley: I would guess that they have little interest in mysteries and they have family enough – with a notable omission, but that's far back in their story.

Was the question of race involved here again? I doubted the Megahys had any white friends and of course, the white world is largely closed off to them, as it is to most black people in the USA. Was their yearning not for me as me, but for me as a white person, to have a real connection to that world?

Probably they had never before been involved so directly with a white man – maybe I'm the only white person they have ever hugged?

I knew Susan's driver, Philippe, very well. He's a Haitian, of mixed race himself, about the same color as my father, and during the day he had taken quite an interest in my story. As we talked on the way back to that other world in Manhattan, on Museum Mile, on Fifth Avenue, several times he expressed curiosity about the same topic, never addressing it directly, but what it boiled down to was that he had some difficulty believing that I was not in the least embarrassed about being related to these black people, and that in fact, I had embraced them so fully and easily. Philippe asked me what my friends thought about it, and I told him that they thought it was fascinating and an exciting development in my life.

Then he told me a story about how an Algerian he knew had been working in Brooklyn with a black construction crew. The Algerian told them he was, like them, an African. They looked at him in disbelief and laughed. Irritated, he showed them his immigration documents, describing him as 'North African'. One of the black men said, 'Hey, this brother *really* is a brother!'

Philippe said, 'Now, with everything you found out about your family, you can claim to be a minority, and get all the benefits!'

We were still laughing at that when we stopped at the grand entrance of the Fifth Avenue apartment and

Philippe got out and held the car door open for me. Flatbush seemed a long way away.

*

There was a surprising coda to my meeting with Aggie. I came back to Los Angeles from New York to find an e-mail from Jenniffer, one of my great-nieces in Kalamazoo.I replied to it, and described my meeting with Aggie in some detail.

The next day, I got a call from Henrymae in Kalamazoo and she told me that Jenniffer had printed my letter and showed it to her. It seemed to have caused her some small anxiety.

'Are you sure this story is true?' she asked me, and then steamed on before I could answer, 'because it doesn't sound right me!'

I told her that I wasn't sure, but if it wasn't, there were some coincidences that would be hard to explain, and that I was going to check it out.

'Good!' she approved, 'that's good, because this doesn't sound like your father!'

'It doesn't..?'

'No, sir. Remember, Robert knew your father very well and he told me time and time again that he was the sweetest, most charming man, very different from my father-in-law, not the kind of man who'd abandon a child. Now if you were telling me that Grandpa Evan had done this with this girl, then I could believe it.'

'It definitely wasn't Evan, Henrymae.'

'How can you be so sure?'

'Because the child was born in 1911 and Evan didn't get his medical degree until 1915,' I explained.

'But this still doesn't sound like your father, to seduce a young girl like that, and then to go and leave her and the baby, does it?'

I had to admit that it didn't. 'But this was when he was twenty-five, Henrymac. This was twelve or more years before Robert met him, and thirty-five years before I really got to know him myself. And there's no proof that he even knew of his child's existence.'

'Well, that may be, but you just check it for yourself, and you let me know!'

Wondering why she was so skeptical, I promised that I would do exactly that. It obviously wasn't racism: she obviously didn't care that Robert was not entirely white, and had repeated to me more than once that her mother had raised to 'bear no prejudice to anybody, whatever their religion or their race.'

As things turned out, I never found any reason to doubt that the St.Lucia/St. Croix Megahys are my family. Getting to know them has enlarged and illuminated my life. I have become very close to all of them, particularly to Jon Francis, whom I always introduce as 'my nephew'. To be strictly accurate, he's my father's great-grandson with a woman not my own mother – a bit of a mouthful for a social introduction. He's a fine young man, who joined the US Navy after he graduated from Georgia Tech, became the highest level of Navy helicopter pilot, served two tours on an aircraft carrier and is currently a Flight Instructor at the Pensacola Flight School.

He's very smart, has a great sense of humor, and in many ways does remind me of my father. Just like my father, his is a quiet strength, he feels no need to impose himself on a social group. Sometimes, he grows a mustache, my father always had a mustache, and I think I see a resemblance between them. Jon Francis and I have spent a lot of time together, in Los Angeles and in New York, and in spite of the enormous differences between us, of age, of life experience and culture, we feel at home in each other's company and I know that he will be a life-long friend.

One day, he wittily pointed out a contrast between his branch of the family and mine. 'Your part of the family has got whiter and whiter,' he said. 'Mine has got darker and darker!'

Skin color, race, is always there, a cloud, a shadow, a fact, a feeling, which somehow can never be entirely dispelled. The St. Croix Megahy's are self-segregated, it's unstated and undiscussed, but there it is. Jon Francis was stationed for a few years in San Diego, and I went down there to a going-away party that his local friends gave for him in the home of a family who had taken him under their wing, a serviceman far from home. There was good food and drink, some of his Navy colleagues were there, and some pretty girls too, of course; all in all, a very congenial evening.

I was the only white guest.

*

In Brooklyn with my half-brother's widow, Aggie Megahy, and his grand daughter, Ashley Megahy

On Mulholland Drive in Beverly Hills, with my half-brother's grandson, whom I found on the internet: Jon Francis Megahy

Having lunch in Beverly Hills with my half-brother's son, Leonard, and his wife, Laureen

On the beach in Mailbu, with Ashley Megahy, her sister Coral, and Jon Francis Megahy

33 Reflections

Now, alongside the clear images and precise memories I have of my father, I have to place a more elusive figure, a man whose inner torments I can only guess at, a man whose goodwill to me is in no doubt, but a man whose life was charted by his social environment to a degree that I can scarcely imagine from the privileged perspective that his deceptions helped to give me.

The discovery that my father was not exactly the person I thought I knew, that he had an agenda controlling his life that I never could have suspected, shattered at a stroke many of my unquestioned lifelong assumptions about myself – but it also revealed the reasons for actions I had undertaken intuitively, and could never quite explain to myself.

I used to think that I knew my father really well, as well as you'd expect to know your father, but now I have had to deal with the painful knowledge that I knew only one version of him. There were so many questions I had to ask myself: why had I never thought it strange that he never spoke of his parents or his early life? And what was my responsibility in all this, why had I never asked him about those subjects? As I began to reach a new understanding of myself, I also tried to find a new evaluation of him and that pernicious force that shaped his life: racism.

It was not until the later part of my life that I discovered that I had a direct, visceral involvement with the issues of race – and it was decades before I found out that my father was not at all what my entire family thought he was, and what I certainly believed him to be. As a young man, he faced agonizing choices: accepting the role the white community assigned to him as a second-class citizen; rebelling against that role; or running away and pretending to be someone else altogether.

He was completely successful in his lifelong deception: his choice of the secret life did create the white family that he so fervently desired; and in his lifetime, his true ancestry was never revealed. He did manage to live the white American Dream; bizarrely, in Essex, England.

It's tempting to wonder what would have happened if he had not been killed in his car that day; what would he have thought as the brave new world of the 1960's got into its stride, when suddenly black was Black Power, when suddenly Black was Beautiful – black, which he'd been running away from all his life? Suddenly blacks were being encouraged not to straighten their hair – suddenly undermining the value of his so-straight hair.

It was hardly possible for him to grow an Afro and declare, 'Hey, I'm a proud black man too!' Of the many sacrifices he had made for his fake life, pride was one of the most painful. To avoid the humiliation of being disdained by whites, he had to surrender to the self-humiliation of denying his true identity.

And yet he certainly was a proud man, proud of his academic accomplishments, of his medical skills, of saving the lives of many patients he had treated in extremis. But still he kept his head down, self-effacing on the outside, and on the inside..? I'll never know, but those decisions he had made in the earlier decades of his life must have come back to haunt him as British society tried to throw off its class and racial shackles.

As he saw his white son scorn racism, reject class-consciousness, embrace friends and acquaintances of all classes and colors, surely he must have thought again and again, What if..? If only...

But by that time, of course, a confession was out of the question. When a man has connected the dots of his real life with fabulous links to form a seamless chain of deceit, has laboriously converted to an alien religion, has so frequently repeated his fictional saga to so many strangers, friends and family members, well, then, how could he possibly go back, return to the real story of his life that he had virtually ceased to believe himself for so many years?

In the 1960's, homosexuals were coming out, but my father was staying in. In, there was security, safety from the still-possible racial taunts and rejections. Whatever changes were bubbling up beneath the surface, Britain was still a society divided by skin-color. The very idea of multi-culturalism, so widely touted in the past few decades, was – and probably always will be – in the future.

Perhaps, if my father had lived just a few years longer, another decade maybe, into the 1970's – which is when most of the real social changes that people think took place in the 60's actually did happen – then perhaps he might have found the courage to break his self-constructed bonds. Perhaps one day he might have sat me down and said to me, 'Son, I'm not exactly the man you think I am...'

It would not have been so easy with my mother. Whatever suspicions and second thoughts may have roamed around her head at some time in their relationship, had been long ago banished or unconsciously accepted. Her deliberate lack of curiosity, her real acceptance of the fake Ken, had made her his accomplice, and in declaring his own falsehoods, he would have been pronouncing her guilty of dishonesty as well.

He must have thought about it, he must have felt tremendous pressure to gain the release of confession. But how would his intimates take it? Would his apparently liberal son turn out to be a closet bigot when confronting his principles of egalitarianism right there in his own home? Would his wife, not exactly a devout Jew, but as ethnically Jew-conscious as it's possible to be, run from the house screaming and shamed? And the Cohen family wailing, 'Oy vey, Sadie's married a *schwartzer*!' It was simply unthinkable.

As for the risk of exposure, his biggest danger there would have come if I'd wanted to travel to the US, and had visited Uncle Evan. My father knew, as we did not, that he might have been able to censor his brother's conversations with me on the verboten subjects in London, but if I went to Chicago, the evidence would be plain for me to see. But in those far-off days when the US was a distant, exotic country, very expensive to visit, he was in no danger of being exposed by me making such a journey.

So, after all, why own up, why face those still-hurtful truths – why gamble with confession? Everything was running along nicely. But what was lost to us, his family, is that where his enterprise failed?

The sense of intimacy I always felt with him was, I

now know, incomplete. Not only on his side; I was holding back too. Somehow I always sensed that there was more to him than I could know, was allowed to know, that there was a mystery to him, but I could never articulate what that mystery was.

His flight into white society, made possible by the genetic accident that gave him straight hair and a light complexion, carried its own penalties – and some of them have been exacted on me. But even today, in a US where you can be arrested for DWB, 'driving while black', could I condemn anyone's decision to escape from those issues? *[35]*

Much less can I condemn my father for running away from a society where life-threatening racism was rampant; where lynching was still commonplace; where the voting rights conferred on the former slaves after a civil war of unparalleled bloodshed, had been systematically and ingeniously torn away; and where the white organization controlling his professional life barred academically qualified blacks from membership.

But that's all history; if my father was alive today, reading about the 'Birthers' persistent denials of Barack Obama's US citizenship, or the Trayvon Martin case, would he think he made the wrong decisions?

If he had been following the 2012 Presidential election, watching the maps analyzed on the news shows, showing how all the states voted, he could have hardly have failed to notice that the southern states which voted against Obama exactly matched the states of the Confederation. Oh yes, he would have seen that one hundred and fifty years after the Confederate states fought to maintain their right to enslave other human beings, those same states had voted against the re-election of a black man to the White House. So can I confidently assert that his decision to 'pass' was wrong?

Racism framed and determined Kenneth Megahy's life as it has framed and determined the lives of millions of others, and his response to it framed and determined my life. 'Passing' has always exacted a toll on those who were able to do it, and on their intimates, but who am I to judge that his life as he lived it in his time was less honorable, less worthwhile, than if he had faced up directly to the many penalties and few privileges of his racial heritage?

Now that I know his great secret, I love him no less, I do not judge him and I still smile when I think of him.

But if only we could have had the opportunity to speak about it; if only he could have had the courage to confide the truth to me, to trust that my love for him was as strong as his for me, that it was strong enough to bear the burden of those truths he ran away from for so long; then I might have been able to ease the burden of his demons by sharing it. I'll always struggle with his choice not to confide in me, in me alone – not in the world.

Maintaining his deceptions was unquestionably in his own self-interest because it preserved his relationship with me and the world, but I'm also sure that he was determined to protect me from whatever stresses and shocks the revelation of his real ancestry might bring with it.

In every possible sense, I know now that I am an immigrant. Although my mother was born in England, in her insulated ghetto she lived her life in a virtually sealed world. I was also born in Hightown, and carried much of its narrowed sensibility with me to the wider worlds I've explored; now, as an American citizen of foreign birth, I'm a different kind of immigrant.

I suppose I was always uncertain where I belonged; it was partly that uncertainty that made me leave England, but it took my discoveries about my father to make me recognize and accept my feeling of being a perpetual outsider.

I have found peace in that acceptance, there are no more dark clouds of a vaguely mysterious past just out of sight of my mind's eye; but of course, my journey of discovery about myself will continue as long as my heart beats.

END

MEGAHY FAMILY TREE

Robert Sheremiah Megahy & Sarah Jane Forte
1829 – 1862
[Married August 3rd 1853 Bridgetown, Barbados]

James Megahy & Frances Anne Brewster [Thorne]
1855 – 1919
[Married May 3rd 1883 Bridgetown, Barbados]

James Kenneth Megahy & Rebecca Joseph
[1911 St.Lucia, never married]

James Kenneth Megahy &
Sarah Cohen
1885 – 1962
[Married 10-6-1933, London
England]

Evan Aubrey Megahy &
Mayme Howard
1893-1970
[Married April 10 1907]

Francis Megahy
18-3-1935

Robert Megahy &
HenryMae Cryer
1912 -1981
[Married 2-15-1949]

St.John Francis Megahy & Aggie William
1909 – 1981
[Married 5-9-1944]

Merry, Patti and Sarajane
Megahy

Leonard Megahy & Laureen Henry
[Married 7-26-1980]

John Francis Megahy, Coral Megahy and Ashley Megahy

SOURCES

This is not an exhaustive list of the sources I consulted, merely some useful sources for the general reader. Each of the subjects dealt with below have been covered by many authors, researchers and publications.

1)   http://www.usatoday.com/news/washington/presidential-approval-tracker.htm

2)   *LA Times, March 12, 2012*
http://articles.latimes.com/2012/mar/12/news/la-pn-poll-obamas-a-muslim-to-many-gop-voters-in-alabama-mississippi-20120312

3)   http://books.google.com/booksid=ek_0OoxYoIC&pg=PA309&lpg=PA309&dq=venezuela+gold+rush&source=bl&ots=WGaLDKNepi&sig=r9DLAxgzmCgf4A-4GOyt5iLiWYE&hl=en&sa=X&ei=TuqhT5_VD6iliQKEwmXBw&ved=0CEMQ6AEwBDgU#v=onepage&q=venezuela%20gold%20rush&f=false

4)   http://www.facebook.com/pages/Harrison-College/144420788905021

5)   http://www.ellisisland.org/search/shipManifest.asp?order_num=1786115428&MID=0750466854002991056o&order_num=1786115428&ORDER_ID=1500036058&LNM=MEGAHY&PLNM=MEGAHY&last_kind=0&RF=9&pID=102532010052&-

6)   http://www.jackwhite.net/iberia/caribbean.html

7)   http://www.funbarbados.com/trust/synagogue.cf
m
8)   http://barbados.gssites.com/pages/info/index
.htm [para 3]
9)   http://jonpat.tripod.com/history.html
10)   http://www.bbc.co.uk/history/british/empire
_seapower/barbados_01.shtml see Abolition

11)   http://www.historyplace.com/worldhistory/f
amine/

12)   Of the four members of the great rock band the
Beatles, three were of Irish descent

13)   http://books.google.com/books?
id=XHtKAAAAMAAJ&printsec=frontcover&dq=inaut
hor:%22David+Augustus+Straker
%22&hl=en&sa=X&ei=0M53T6adB-
akiQKgsbmnDg&ved=0CEIQ6AEwAQ#v=onepage&q
=inauthor%3A%22David%20Augustus%20Straker
%22&f=false

14)   David Slone's groundbreaking book, Buried in
the Bitter Waters

15)   April 26 1937:
http://www.time.com/time/magazine/article/0,9171,
757674-2,00.html

16)   Per Ronald L. F. Davis, Ph. D., California State
University, Northridge

17)   http://www.tampabay.com/news/publicsafet
y/crime/trayvon-martin-a-typical-teen-with-dreams-
of-flying-or-fixing-planes/1221425

18)   Encyclopedia of American race riots: By
Walter C. Rucker, James N. Upton
http://books.google.com/books?
id=mQcrpqn0124C&pg=PA475&lpg=PA475&dq=New
+York+tenderloin+riot&source=bl&ots=y5sdXm0slw
&sig=dElk7-waQMc3UcU5HAXpMTp2ioI&hl=en&ei=-
PyUTqyfG6rX0QH-

meGMCA&sa=X&oi=book_result&ct=result&resnum=
6&ved=0CD4Q6AEwBTgU#v=onepage&q=New
%20York%20tenderloin%20riot&f=false

19) http://dawnontheamazon.com/blog/2011/09/21/st
eamships-of-the-rubber-boom-recovering-history-in-the-
peruvian-amazon/

20) http://books.google.com/books?
id=XHtKAAAAMAAJ&printsec=frontcover&dq=inauthor
:%22David+Augustus+Straker
%22&hl=en&sa=X&ei=0M53T2adB-
akiQKgsbmnDg&ved=0CEIQ6AEwAQ#v=onepage&q=in
author%3A%22David%20Augustus%20Straker
%22&f=false

21) Ibid

22) http://www.amaapology.com/news16.html

23) Lawrence J. Friedman,: The White Savage: Racial
Fantasies in the Postbellum South

24) http://blackhistorycanada.ca/timeline.php?
id=1800 Also: http://www.google.com/url?
sa=t&rct=j&q=&esrc=s&source=web&cd=4&ved=0CEYQ
FjAD&url=http%3A%2F
%2Fwww.nationalarchives.gov.uk%2Fpathways
%2Fblackhistory%2Frights
%2Fslave_free.htm&ei=w9J3T5HfIKf9iQL_srSnDg&usg
=AFQjCNF_phohOTy0XKILAFhN1yE5b-
X4rQ&sig2=HFyfFtWokUqDfW95og4EJQ

25) Douglass.
http://www.yale.edu/glc/archive/1091.htm

26) Donnet-Zedel –
http://www.ccarshow.net/index.php?
page=http://www.ccarshow.net/carmake.php?
menu=1&make=1214/

27) www.movinghere.org.uk/galleries/histories/jewish
/settling/manchester_jewry_2.htm#

Conversion - http://www.convertingtojudaism.com/

28) http://www.google.com/imgres?
imgurl=http://www.whitehavenandwesternlakeland.co.uk
/vintage2009/v-
morris8.jpg&imgrefurl=http://www.whitehavenandwestc
rnlakeland.co.uk/vintage2009/vintage.htm&h=352&w=50
0&sz=85&tbnid=8BC5U7Vlzm8zSM:&tbnh=90&tbnw=128
&zoom=1&docid=DByyJtJXUDk9VM&sa=X&ei=UPmhT4_
cCaGxiQKVjsG-Bw&ved=0CDcQ9QEwBQ&

29) http://www.car-
brochures.eu/roveradverts.htm#667001809 AND
http://en.wikipedia.org/wiki/File:1938_Rover_14.JPG

30) http://www.spartacus.schoolnet.co.uk/2WWbritain
B.htm

31) [20 August 1940] "The gratitude of every home in
our Island, in our Empire, and indeed throughout the
world, except in the abodes of the guilty, goes out to the
British airmen who, undaunted by odds, unwearied in their
constant challenge and mortal danger, are turning the tide
of the World War by their prowess and by their devotion.
Never in the field of human conflict was so much owed by
so many to so few. All our hearts go out to the fighter pilots,
whose brilliant actions we see with our own eyes day after
day..."

32) http://www.history.army.mil/html/topics/afam/a
a-volinfreps.html

33) http://www.ww2talk.com/forum/united-
kingdom/21458-ww2-petrol-rationing.html

34) http://www.huffingtonpost.com/2011/12/08/racial
-traffic-stop-disparity_n_1137656.html

44116387R00179

Made in the USA
Lexington, KY
22 August 2015